THE
IDEA OF NAT

THE
IDEA OF NATURE

R. G. COLLINGWOOD

OXFORD UNIVERSITY PRESS

LONDON   OXFORD   NEW YORK

First published by the Clarendon Press, 1945
First issued as an Oxford University Press paperback, 1960
This reprint 1978
Printed in the United States of America

OXFORD UNIVERSITY PRESS
Oxford   London   Glasgow
New York   Toronto   Melbourne   Wellington
Ibadan   Nairobi   Dar es Salaam   Cape Town
Kuala Lumpur   Singapore   Jakarta   Hong Kong   Tokyo
Delhi   Bombay   Calcutta   Madras   Karachi

PREFATORY NOTE

WHEN his *Essay on Philosophical Method* was passing through the press in 1933 Collingwood remarked to a friend that, having propounded a theory of philosophical method, he was now proceeding to apply it to a problem which had never been solved, namely, to the Philosophy of Nature. From August 1933 to September 1934 he was working intensively at this subject, studying the history of both natural science and cosmological speculation, and elaborating a cosmology of his own. It is the work done at that time which forms the substance of this book.

The material then accumulated in his note-books was condensed into lectures delivered in the Michaelmas Term 1934 and again in 1937. In September 1939 the manuscript of the lectures was drastically revised and a beginning was made on rewriting it in book form for publication. At a later date, although he was then mainly occupied with *The New Leviathan*, Collingwood found time to revise his work a little further, notably the section on Hegel, and he then substituted the short concluding passage on the transition from Nature to History for the sketch of his own cosmology which had closed the original lectures and with which he may have become dissatisfied.

At his death the manuscript had been completely prepared for publication down to the end of Part I, Chapter 1, but no farther. Nevertheless, little editing of the remainder has been required: chapter and section divisions have been inserted; certain traces of the lecture form have been removed; and minor points of detail have been corrected. No attempt has been made to construct the more extensive documentation which Collingwood intended to provide for the passage on Pythagoras and perhaps elsewhere.

The editor's thanks are due to Mr. F. Sherwood Taylor, to Professor E. A. Milne for the footnote on page 153, and to Professor H. H. Price for many helpful suggestions.

T. M. K.

25 *May* 1944.

CONTENTS

CONTENTS

PART III. THE MODERN VIEW OF NATURE

INTRODUCTION

§ 1. *Science and Philosophy*

IN the history of European thought there have been three periods of constructive cosmological thinking; three periods, that is to say, when the idea of nature has come into the focus of thought, become the subject of intense and protracted reflection, and consequently acquired new characteristics which in their turn have given a new aspect to the detailed science of nature that has been based upon it.

To say that the detailed science of nature is 'based' upon the idea of nature does not imply that the idea of nature in general, the idea of nature as a whole, is worked out first, in abstraction from any detailed study of natural fact, and that when this abstract idea of nature is complete people go on to erect upon it a superstructure of detailed natural science. What it implies is not a temporal relation but a logical one. Here, as often, the temporal relation inverts the logical relation. In natural science, as in economics or morals or law, people begin with the details. They begin by tackling individual problems as they arise. Only when this detail has accumulated to a considerable amount do they reflect upon the work they have been doing and discover that they have been doing it in a methodical way, according to principles of which hitherto they have not been conscious.

But the temporal priority of detailed work to reflection on the principles implied in it must not be exaggerated. It would be an exaggeration, for example, to think that a 'period' of detailed work in natural science, or any other field of thought or action, a 'period' lasting for half a century or even for half a decade, is followed by a 'period' of reflection on the principles which logically underlie it. Such a contrast between 'periods' of non-philosophical thinking and subsequent 'periods' of philosophizing is perhaps what Hegel meant to assert in his famous lament, at the end of the Preface to the *Philosophie des Rechts*: 'When philosophy paints its grey in grey, a form of life has aged; and grey in grey does not enable us to make it young again, but only to know it. The owl of Minerva begins to fly only at the coming of dusk.' If that was what Hegel meant, he made a mistake: and a mistake which Marx only turned upside down and did not correct when he wrote that 'philosophy hitherto has confined itself to interpreting the world: the point, however, is to change it' (*Theses on Feuerbach*, xi). The complaint against philosophy is borrowed, in the very same words, from Hegel; only what Hegel represents as a necessary feature of all philosophy Marx represents as a defect to which philosophy was subject until he, Marx, revolutionized it.

In fact, the detailed work seldom goes on for any length of time without reflection intervening. And this reflection reacts upon the detailed work; for when people become conscious of the principles upon which they have been thinking or acting they become conscious of something which in these thoughts and actions they have been trying, though unconsciously, to do: namely to work out in detail the logical implications of those principles. To strong minds this new consciousness gives a new strength, namely a new firmness in their approach to the detailed problems. To weak minds it adds a new temptation, the temptation to that kind of pedantry which consists in remembering the principle and forgetting the special features of the problem to which it is applied.

The detailed study of natural fact is commonly called natural science, or for short simply science; the reflection on principles, whether those of natural science or of any other department of thought or action, is commonly called philosophy. Talking in these terms, and restricting philosophy for the moment to reflection on the principles of natural science, what I have just said may be put by saying that natural science must come first in order that philosophy may have something to reflect on; but that the two things are so closely related that natural science cannot go on for long without philosophy beginning; and that philosophy reacts on the science out of which it has grown by giving it in future a new firmness and consistency arising out of the scientist's new consciousness of the principles on which he has been working.

For this reason it cannot be well that natural science should be assigned exclusively to one class of persons called scientists and philosophy to another class called philosophers. A man who has never reflected on the principles of his work has not achieved a grown-up man's attitude towards it; a scientist who has never philosophized about his science can never be more than a second-hand, imitative, journeyman scientist. A man who has never enjoyed a certain type of experience cannot reflect upon it;

a philosopher who has never studied and worked at natural science cannot philosophize about it without making a fool of himself.

Before the nineteenth century the more eminent and distinguished scientists at least had always to some extent philosophized about their science, as their writings testify. And inasmuch as they regarded natural science as their main work, it is reasonable to assume that these testimonies understate the extent of their philosophizing. In the nineteenth century a fashion grew up of separating natural scientists and philosophers into two professional bodies, each knowing little about the other's work and having little sympathy with it. It is a bad fashion that has done harm to both sides, and on both sides there is an earnest desire to see the last of it and to bridge the gulf of misunderstanding it has created. The bridge must be begun from both ends; and I, as a member of the philosophical profession, can best begin at my end by philosophizing about what experience I have of natural science. Not being a professional scientist, I know that I am likely to make a fool of myself; but the work of bridge-building must go on.

§ 2. *The Greek view of nature*

Greek natural science was based on the principle that the world of nature is saturated or permeated by mind. Greek thinkers regarded the presence of mind in nature as the source of that regularity or orderliness in the natural world whose presence made a science of nature possible. The world of nature they regarded as a world of bodies in motion. The motions in themselves, according to Greek ideas, were due to vitality or 'soul'; but motion in itself is one thing, they believed, and orderliness another. They conceived mind, in all its manifestations, whether in human affairs or elsewhere, as a ruler, a dominating or regulating element, imposing order first upon itself and then upon everything belonging to it, primarily its own body and secondarily that body's environment.

Since the world of nature is a world not only of ceaseless motion and therefore alive, but also a world of orderly or regular motion, they accordingly said that the world of nature is not only alive but intelligent; not only a vast animal with a 'soul' or life of its own, but a rational animal with a 'mind' of its own. The life and intelligence of creatures inhabiting the earth's surface and the regions adjacent to it, they argued, represent a specialized local organization of this all-pervading vitality and rationality, so that a plant or animal, according to their ideas, participates in its own degree psychically in the life-process of the world's 'soul' and intellectually in the activity of the world's 'mind', no less than it participates materially in the physical organization of the world's 'body'.

That vegetables and animals are physically akin to the earth is a belief shared by ourselves with the Greeks; but the notion of a psychical and intellectual kinship is strange to us, and constitutes a difficulty in the way of our understanding the relics of Greek natural science which we find in their literature.

§ 3. *The Renaissance view of Nature*

The second of the three cosmological movements mentioned at the beginning of this chapter took place in the sixteenth and seventeenth centuries. I propose to designate its view of nature by the náme of 'Renaissance' cosmology. The name is not a good one, because the word 'Renaissance' is applied to an earlier phase in the history of thought, beginning in Italy with the humanism of the fourteenth century and continuing, in the same country, with the Platonic and Aristotelian cosmologies of that century and the fifteenth. The cosmology I have now to describe was in principle a reaction against these and might, perhaps, be more accurately called 'post-Renaissance'; but this is a clumsy term.

Historians of art have lately been using, for some part of the period with which I am concerned, the adjective 'baroque'; but this is a word borrowed from the technicalities of formal logic as a term of contempt for a certain kind of bad taste prevalent in the seventeenth century, and its adoption as a descriptive epithet for the natural science of Galileo, Descartes, and Newton would be 'bien baroque'.[1] The word 'gothic', as applied to medieval architecture, succeeded in divesting itself of its original significance and becoming a term merely descriptive of a certain style; but no one, I think, ever proposed to call

---

[1] Saint-Simon, *apud* Littré, quoted in Croce, *Storia della Età barocca in Italia* (Bari, 1928), p. 22. Cf. *Encyclopédie*: 'L'idée du baroque entraîne avec soi celle du ridicule poussé à l'excès.' And Francesco Milizia, *Dizionario delle belle arti del disegno* (1797): 'Barocco è il superlativo del bizzarro, l'eccesso del ridicolo.' Both quoted in Croce, op. cit., p. 23.

the work of Aquinas or Scotus 'gothic philosophy'; and even as applied to architecture the term is now disappearing. So I shall use the term 'Renaissance', with this definition of my meaning and this apology for departing from established usage.

The Renaissance view of nature began to take shape as antithetical to the Greek view in the work of Copernicus (1473–1543), Telesio (1508–88), and Bruno (1548–1600). The central point of this antithesis was the denial that the world of nature, the world studied by physical science, is an organism, and the assertion that it is devoid both of intelligence and of life. It is therefore incapable of ordering its own movements in a rational manner, and indeed incapable of moving itself at all. The movements which it exhibits, and which the physicist investigates, are imposed upon it from without, and their regularity is due to 'laws of nature' likewise imposed from without. Instead of being an organism, the natural world is a machine: a machine in the literal and proper sense of the word, an arrangement of bodily parts designed and put together and set going for a definite purpose by an intelligent mind outside itself. The Renaissance thinkers, like the Greeks, saw in the orderliness of the natural world an expression of intelligence: but for the Greeks this intelligence was nature's own intelligence, for the Renaissance thinkers it was the intelligence of something other than nature: the divine creator and ruler of nature. This distinction is the key to all the main differences between Greek and Renaissance natural science.

Each of these cosmological movements was followed by a movement in which the focus of interest shifted from nature to mind. In the history of Greek thought this shift took place with Socrates. Whereas previous thinkers had not neglected ethics, politics, or even logic and the theory of knowledge, they had concentrated their main effort of thought upon the theory of nature. Socrates reversed this emphasis and concentrated his thought on ethics and logic; and from his time onwards, although the theory of nature was by no means forgotten even by Plato, who did far more work on that subject than is generally realized, the theory of mind predominated, and the theory of nature took the second place.

This Greek theory of mind in Socrates and his successors was intimately connected with and conditioned by the results already obtained in the theory of nature. The mind that was

studied by Socrates, Plato, and Aristotle was always first and
foremost mind *in* nature, the mind in the body and of the body,
manifesting itself by its control of the body; and when these
philosophers found themselves obliged to recognize mind as
transcending body, they stated this discovery in a way that
shows unmistakably how paradoxical it seemed to them and
how remote from their habitual or (as we sometimes say)
'instinctive' ways of thinking. Socrates in Plato's dialogues
over and over again expects to be met with incredulity and
misunderstanding when he sets out to assert that rational soul
or mind operates independently of the body: either when he is
discussing the theory of knowledge and contrasts the bodily
mind of appetite and sense with the pure intellectual apprehension of the forms which is effected by the rational soul's
wholly independent and self-contained activity without any
help from the body, or when he is expounding the doctrine of
immortality and asserting that the rational soul enjoys an
eternal life unaffected by the birth or death of the body
belonging to it.

The same tone is found in Aristotle, who treats it as a matter
of course that the 'soul' should be defined as the entelechy of
an organic body—that is, the self-maintaining activity of an
organism—but speaks as one expounding mysterious and
difficult doctrine when he says that the intellect or reason, νοῦς,
although in some sense it is a part of the 'soul', possesses no
bodily organ and is not acted upon, as sense is, by its proper
objects (*De Anima* 429ᵃ15 seqq.) so that it is nothing apart from
its activity of thinking (ibid. 21–2) and is 'separable' from the
body (ibid. 429ᵇ5). All this shows what from a general knowledge
of pre-Socratic physics we should expect: that Greek thinkers in
general take it for granted that mind belongs essentially to body
and lives with it in the closest union, and that when they are
confronted with reasons for thinking this union partial, occa-
sional, or precarious, they are puzzled to know how this can be.

In Renaissance thought this state of things is precisely
reversed. For Descartes body is one substance and mind is
another. Each works independently of the other according to
its own laws. Just as the fundamental axiom of Greek thought
about mind is its immanence in body, so the fundamental
axiom of Descartes is its transcendence. Descartes knows very

well that transcendence must not be pushed to the point of dualism; the two things must be connected somehow; but cosmologically he can find no connexion short of God, and in the individual human being he is driven to the desperate expedient, justly ridiculed by Spinoza, of finding it in the pineal gland, which he thinks must be the organ of union between body and soul because, as an anatomist, he can find no other function for it.

Even Spinoza, with his insistence on the unity of substance, is in no better case; for thought and extension are in his philosophy two utterly distinct attributes of this one substance, and each, as an attribute, completely transcends the other. Hence when in the eighteenth century the centre of gravity in philosophical thought swung over from the theory of nature to the theory of mind, Berkeley being the critical point here as Socrates was for the Greeks, the problem of nature inevitably stated itself in this form: how can mind have any connexion with something utterly alien to itself, something essentially mechanical and non-mental, namely nature? This was the question, at bottom the only question, concerning nature which exercised the great philosophers of mind, Berkeley, Hume, Kant, Hegel. In every case their answer was at bottom the same: namely, that mind makes nature; nature is, so to speak, a by-product of the autonomous and self-existing activity of mind.

I shall discuss this idealistic view of nature more fully here-after; all I wish to make clear at this point is that there are two things which it never meant. It never meant that nature is in itself mental, made of the stuff of mind; on the contrary, it set out from the assumption that nature is radically non-mental or mechanical, and never went back on that assumption, but always maintained that nature is essentially alien to mind, mind's other or opposite. Secondly it never meant that nature is an illusion or dream of mind, something non-existent: on the contrary, it always maintained that nature really is what it seems to be: it is the work of mind and not existing in its own right, but a work really produced and, because really produced, really existing.

A warning against these two errors is needed because they have been over and over again taught as truths in modern books whose authors are so much obsessed by the ideas of the twentieth century that they simply cannot understand those of the eighteenth. They are, in a way, none the worse for this; it is progress, of a sort, that people should have got right away from the thoughts of their great-grandfathers; but that is not a kind of progress which qualifies people for making historical statements about the ideas which they have ceased to understand; and when they venture to make such statements, and to say that for Hegel 'material characteristics are delusive appearances of certain mental characteristics' (C. D. Broad, *The Mind and its Place in Nature*, 1928, p. 624) or that according to Berkeley 'experience of green is entirely indistinguishable from green' (G. E. Moore, *Philosophical Studies*, 1922, p. 14, where Berkeley is not named, but seems to be meant) respect for their personal attainments and their academic positions must not blind a reader to the fact that they are publishing untrue statements about something they have not understood.

The Greek view of nature as an intelligent organism was based on an analogy: an analogy between the world of nature and the individual human being, who begins by finding certain characteristics in himself as an individual, and goes on to think of nature as possessed of similar characteristics. By the work of his own self-consciousness he comes to think of himself as a body whose parts are in constant rhythmic motion, these motions being delicately adjusted to each other so as to preserve the vitality of the whole: and at the same time he finds himself to be a mind directing the activity of this body in accordance with its own desires. The world of nature as a whole is then explained as a macrocosm analogous to this microcosm.

The Renaissance view of nature as a machine is equally analogical in its origin, but it presupposes a quite different order of ideas. First, it is based on the Christian idea of a creative and omnipotent God. Secondly, it is based on the human experience of designing and constructing machines. The Greeks and Romans were not machine-users, except to a very small extent: their catapults and water-clocks were not a prominent enough feature of their life to affect the way in which they conceived the relation between themselves and the world. But by the sixteenth century the Industrial Revolution was well on the way. The printing-press and the windmill, the lever, the pump, and the pulley, the clock and the wheelbarrow, and a host of machines in use among miners and engineers were established features of daily life. Everyone understood the nature of a machine, and the experience of making and using such things had become part of the general consciousness of European man. It was an easy step to the proposition: as a clockmaker or millwright is to a clock or mill, so is God to Nature.

§ 4. *The Modern view of Nature*

The modern view of Nature owes something both to Greek and to Renaissance cosmology, but it differs from each in fundamental ways. To describe the differences with precision is not easy, because the movement is still young and has not yet had the time to ripen its ideas for systematic statement. We are confronted not so much with a new cosmology as with a large number of new cosmological experiments, all very disconcerting if looked at from the Renaissance point of view, and all to some extent animated by what we can recognize as a single spirit; but to define this spirit is very difficult. We can, however, describe the kind of experience on which it is based, and so indicate the starting-point of this movement.

Modern cosmology, like its predecessors, is based on an analogy. What is new about it is that the analogy is a new one. As Greek natural science was based on the analogy between the macrocosm nature and the microcosm man, as man is revealed to himself in his own self-consciousness; as Renaissance natural science was based on the analogy between nature as God's handiwork and the machines that are the handiwork of man (the same *Analogy* which in the eighteenth century was to become the presupposition of Joseph Butler's masterpiece[1]); so the modern view of nature, which first begins to find expression towards the end of the eighteenth century and ever since then has been gathering weight and establishing itself more securely down to the present day, is based on the analogy between the processes of the natural world as studied by natural scientists and the vicissitudes of human affairs as studied by historians.

Like the Renaissance analogy, this could only begin to operate

[1] 'This method then . . . being evidently conclusive . . . my design is to apply it . . . *taking for proved, that there is an intelligent Author of Nature*' (my italics); op. cit., Introduction, paragraph 10 (Oxford ed., 1897, p. 10).

when certain conditions were fulfilled. Renaissance cosmology, as I have pointed out, arose from a widespread familiarity with the making and handling of machines. The sixteenth century was the time when this familiarity had been achieved. Modern cosmology could only have arisen from a widespread familiarity with historical studies, and in particular with historical studies of the kind which placed the conception of process, change, development in the centre of their picture and recognized it as the fundamental category of historical thought. This kind of history appeared for the first time about the middle of the eighteenth century.[1] Bury finds it first in Turgot (*Discours sur l'histoire universelle*, 1750) and Voltaire (*Le Siècle de Louis XIV*, 1751). It was developed in the *Encyclopédie* (1751–65), and thereafter became a commonplace. Transposed during the next half-century into terms of natural science, the idea of 'progress' became (as in Erasmus Darwin, *Zoonomia*, 1794–8, and Lamarck, *Philosophie zoologique*, 1809) the idea which in another half-century was to become famous as that of 'evolution'.

In its narrowest sense, evolution means the doctrine especially associated with the name of Charles Darwin, though not first expounded by him, that the species of living organisms are not a fixed repertory of permanent types, but begin to exist and cease to exist in time. But this doctrine is only one expression of a tendency which may work, and has in fact worked, in a much wider field: the tendency to resolve the very ancient dualism between changing and unchanging elements in the world of nature by maintaining that what had hitherto been regarded as unchanging was itself in reality subject to change. When this tendency works unchecked, and the conception of unchanging elements in nature is completely eradicated, the result may be called 'radical evolutionism': a doctrine which hardly arrived at maturity until the twentieth century, and was first systematically expounded by Bergson.

The origin of this tendency, which can be traced at work in various fields of natural science for more than a hundred years before Bergson, must be sought in the historical movement of the late eighteenth century, and its further development in the growth of the same movement in the nineteenth.

The concept of evolution, as those who witnessed its detailed

[1] J. B. Bury, *The Idea of Progress* (1924), ch. VII.

application by Darwin to the field of biology knew, marked a crisis of the first importance in the history of human thought. But the earliest attempts at a philosophical exposition of the concept, notably Herbert Spencer's, were amateurish and inconclusive; and the criticism which they justly provoked led not so much to a closer inquiry into the concept itself as to a belief that no such inquiry was worth making.

The question at issue was a very far-reaching one: under what conditions is knowledge possible? For the Greeks it had been an axiom that nothing is knowable unless it is unchanging. The world of nature, again according to the Greeks, is a world of continual and all-pervading change. It might seem to follow that a science of nature is impossible. But Renaissance cosmology had avoided this conclusion by a *distinguo*. The world of nature as it appears to our senses was admitted to be unknowable; but it was argued that behind this world of so-called 'secondary qualities' there lay other things, the true objects of natural science, knowable because unchanging. First, there was the 'substance' or 'matter', itself not subject to change, whose changing arrangements and dispositions were the realities whose appearances to our sensibility took the shape of secondary qualities. Secondly, there were the 'laws' according to which these arrangements and dispositions changed. These two things, matter and natural law, were the unchanging objects of natural science.

What is the relation between the 'matter' which was regarded as the substrate of the changes in the perceptible natural world and the 'laws' according to which those changes took place? Without at all fully discussing this question, I will venture to suggest that they represent the same thing said twice over. The motive for asserting either of them arises from the supposed need for an unchanging and therefore, according to the time-honoured axiom, knowable something behind the changing and therefore unknowable show of nature as we perceive it through our senses.

This changeless something was sought in two directions at once, or (if you will) described in two vocabularies at once. First it was sought by stripping away from nature-as-we-perceive-it whatever is obviously changeable, so as to leave a residue in the shape of a natural world now at last knowable because exempt from change; secondly, it was sought by looking for unchanging relations between the changeables. Alternatively, you may say that the unchangeable something was described first in the vocabulary of 'materialism', as by the early Ionians and secondly in the vocabulary of 'idealism', as by the Pythagoreans; where 'materialism' means the attempt to understand things by asking what they are made of, and 'idealism' the attempt to understand things by asking what 'A is made of B' means: that is, what 'form' has been imposed on it to differentiate it from that out of which it is made.

If the required 'changeless something' can be found in one of these quests, or described in one of these vocabularies, the other becomes unnecessary. Hence 'materialism' and 'idealism', which in the seventeenth century existed peacefully side by side, revealed themselves gradually in the eighteenth century as rivals. To Spinoza it seemed clear that nature revealed itself to the human intellect in two 'attributes', 'extension' and 'thought': where 'extension' means not the visible extension of, for example, visible patches of colour in sky, trees, grass, and so on, but the intelligible 'extension' of geometry, which Descartes had identified with 'matter'; and where 'thought' means not the mental activity of thinking but the 'laws of nature' which are the objects of the natural scientist's thinking. The reality of nature, Spinoza maintains, is alternatively 'expressed' in these two 'attributes'; in other words, Spinoza is 'materialist' and 'idealist' at once. But when Locke maintained that there is 'no science of Substance', he was abandoning the 'materialist' answer to the question and proclaiming the sufficiency of the 'idealist' answer. The question was: How are we to find a changeless and therefore knowable something in, or behind, or somehow belonging to, the flux of nature-as-we-perceive-it? In modern or evolutionary natural science, this question does not arise, and the controversy between 'materialism' and 'idealism', as two answers to it, no longer has any meaning.

This controversy became meaningless because its presuppositions had undergone a revolutionary change by the beginning of the nineteenth century. By then historians had trained themselves to think, and had found themselves able to think scientifically, about a world of constantly changing human affairs in which there was no unchanging substrate behind the changes, and no unchanging laws according to which the changes took place. History had by now established itself as a science, that is, a progressive inquiry in which conclusions are solidly and demonstratively established. It had thus been proved by experiment that scientific knowledge was possible concerning objects that were constantly changing. Once more, the self-consciousness of man, in this case the corporate self-consciousness of man, his historical consciousness of his own corporate doings, provided a clue to his thoughts about nature. The historical conception of scientifically knowable change or process was applied, under the name of evolution, to the natural world.

§ 5. *Consequences of this view*

This new conception of nature, the evolutionary conception based on the analogy of history, has certain characteristics which follow necessarily from the central idea on which it is based. It may be useful to mention a few of them.

i. *Change no longer cyclical, but progressive.* The first to which I will refer is that change takes on, in the mind of the natural scientist, a new character. Greek, Renaissance, and modern thinkers have all agreed that everything in the world of nature, as we perceive it, is in a state of continuous change. But Greek thinkers regarded these natural changes as at bottom always cyclical. A change from a state α to a state β, they thought, is always one part of a process which completes itself by a return from state β to state α. When they found themselves forced to recognize the existence of a change that was not cyclical because it admitted of no such return, e.g. in the change from youth to age in an animal or vegetable organism, they regarded it as a mutilated fragment of a change which, had it been complete, would have been cyclical; and the thing which exhibited it, whether animal or vegetable or anything else, they regarded as defective for that very reason, as not exhibiting in its changes that cyclic pattern which ideally all change ought to show. Alternatively, it was often possible to regard a non-cyclical change not as incomplete in itself but as incompletely known; as a case of cyclical change where for some reason we could perceive only one part of the revolution. This tendency to conceive change as at bottom, or when it is able to realize and exhibit its proper nature *qua* change, not progressive (where by progress I mean a change always leading to something new, with no necessary implication of betterment) but cyclical, was characteristic of the Greek mind throughout its history. I will quote only one striking example of it: the doctrine which haunts Greek cosmology from the Ionians to Aristotle, that the total movement of the world-organism, the movement from which all other movements in the natural world are derived, is a uniform rotation.

Modern thought reverses this state of things. Dominated by the idea of progress or development, which is derived from the principle that history never repeats itself, it regards the world of nature as a second world in which nothing is repeated, a second world of progress characterized, no less than that of history, by the constant emergence of new things. Change is at bottom progressive. Changes that appear to be cyclical are not really cyclical. It is always possible to explain them as cyclical in appearance only, and in reality progressive, in either of two ways: subjectively, by saying that what have been taken for identicals are only similars, or objectively, by saying (to speak metaphorically) that what has been taken for a rotary or circular movement is in fact a spiral movement, one in which the radius is constantly changing or the centre constantly displaced, or both.

ii. *Nature no longer mechanical.* A negative result of introducing the idea of evolution into natural science was the abandonment of the mechanical conception of nature.

It is impossible to describe one and the same thing in the same breath as a machine and as developing or evolving. Something which is developing may build itself machines, but it cannot be a machine. On the evolutionary theory, therefore, there may be machines in nature, but nature cannot itself be a machine, and cannot be either described as a whole or completely described as to any of its parts in mechanical terms.

A machine is essentially a finished product or closed system. Until it is finished it is not a machine. While it is being built it is not functioning as a machine; it cannot do that until it is complete; therefore it can never develop, for developing means working at becoming what as yet one is not (as, for example, a kitten works at growing into a cat), and a machine in an unfinished state cannot work at anything. The only kind of change which a machine can produce in itself by its functioning is breaking down or wearing out. This is not a case of development, because it is not an acquisition of any new functions, it is only a loss of old ones. Thus a steamship in working order can do all the things a broken-down one can do and others besides. A machine may bring about a kind of development in that on which it works, as a grain elevator may build a heap of grain; but if the machine is to go on working this development must be cancelled in the next phase (e.g. the heap must be cleared away), and a cycle of phases substituted for the development.

iii. *Teleology reintroduced.* A positive corollary of this negative result is the reintroduction into natural science of an idea which the mechanical view of nature had banished: the idea of teleology. If the world of nature is a machine or a collection of machines, everything that happens in it is due to 'efficient causes', not in the Aristotelian sense of that Aristotelian phrase but in the mechanistic sense, as denoting impact, attraction, repulsion, and so on. It is only when we discuss the relation of the machine to its maker that 'final causes' begin to appear. If nature is regarded as a machine, then teleology or final causation, with the attendant idea of 'nisus' or effort on the part of nature or something in nature towards the realization of something not yet existing, must be ruled out of natural science altogether; its proper application is to the sphere of mind; to apply it to nature is to confuse the characteristics of these two radically different things.

This negation of teleology in mechanistic natural science may undergo a qualification more apparent than real by contending, as Spinoza did in fact contend, that everything in nature makes an effort to maintain itself in its own being ('in suo esse perseverare conatur', *Ethics*, iii, prop. 6). This is only a quasi-teleology, because the *conatus* of which Spinoza writes is not directed towards the realization of anything not yet existing. Under a form of words which seems to assert the reality and universality of effort, the very essence of effort is in fact denied.

For an evolutionary science of nature, the *esse* of anything in nature is its *fieri*; and a science of that kind must therefore

replace Spinoza's proposition by the proposition that everything in nature tries to persevere in its own becoming: to continue the process of development in which, so far as it exists at
all, it is already engaged. And this contradicts what Spinoza
meant to say; for the 'being' of a thing, in Spinoza, means
what it now is; and a thing engaged in a process of development
is engaged in ceasing to be what it now is, e.g. a kitten, to
become what it now is not, e.g. a cat.

iv. *Substance resolved into function.* The principle that the
esse of a thing is its *fieri* requires a somewhat extensive reform
in the vocabulary of natural science, such that all words and
phrases descriptive of substance or structure shall be replaced
by words and phrases descriptive of function. A mechanistic
science of nature will already possess a considerable vocabulary
of functional terms, but these will always be accompanied by
another vocabulary of structural terms. In any machine
structure is one thing, function another; for a machine has
to be constructed before it can be set in motion.

In order to make a bearing you choose a piece of steel having
a certain degree of hardness, and before it can function as a
bearing you work it to a certain shape. Its size, shape, weight,
hardness, and so forth are structural properties independent of
its acting in this particular machine, or in any other machine,
as a bearing or indeed as anything else. They remain the same
whether or not the machine to which it belongs is in motion or at
rest. Further, these structural properties belonging to a given
part of a given machine, are the foundation and pre-requisite of
its functional properties. Unless the piece of steel has the right
shape, hardness, &c., it will not serve as a bearing.

If nature is a machine, therefore, the various motions of its
parts will be motions of things which have structural properties
of their own independent of these motions and serving as their
indispensable prerequisites. To sum this up: in a machine, and
therefore in nature if nature is mechanical, structure and function are distinct, and function presupposes structure.

In the world of human affairs as known to the historian there
is no such distinction and *a fortiori* no such priority. Structure
is resolvable into function. There is no harm in historians
talking about the structure of feudal society or of capitalist
industry or of the Greek city state, but the reason why there is

no harm in it is because they know that these so-called structures are really complexes of function, kinds of ways in which human beings behave; and that when we say that, for example, the British constitution exists, what we mean is that certain people are behaving in a certain kind of way.

On an evolutionary view of nature a logically constructed natural science will follow the example of history and resolve the structures with which it is concerned into function. Nature will be understood as consisting of processes, and the existence of any special kind of thing in nature will be understood as meaning that processes of a special kind are going on there. Thus 'hardness' in steel will be understood, as in fact it is by modern physicists, not as the name for a structural property of the steel independent of, and presupposed by, any special way in which the steel may behave, but as the name for a way in which it behaves: for example, the name for a rapid movement of the particles composing it, whereby these violently bombard anything that is brought into what is called 'contact' with the steel, that is, within range of the bombardment.

v. *Minimum space and minimum time.* This resolution of structure into function has important consequences for the detail of natural science. Since the conception of any kind of natural substance is resolved into the conception of some kind of natural function; and since these functions are still conceived by natural scientists in the way in which they have been conceived ever since the dawn of Greek thought, namely, as movements; and since any movement occupies space and takes time; it follows that a given kind of natural substance can exist, according to the doctrines of an evolutionary natural science, only in an appropriate amount of space and during an appropriate amount of time. Let us take these two qualifications separately.

(a) *The principle of minimum space.* An evolutionary natural science will maintain that a given kind of natural substance can exist only in an appropriate amount of space. It is not infinitely divisible. There is a smallest possible quantity of it; and if that quantity is divided the parts are not specimens of that kind of substance.

This is the doctrine propounded by John Dalton early in the nineteenth century, and now universally accepted. It is called atomism, but it differs no less from the doctrine of the Greek atomists than it does from the homoeomerism of Anaxagoras. Anaxagoras held that specific natural substances were made up of particles homogeneous with themselves, and any such idea as this is in obvious conflict with Daltonian chemistry, according to which water, for example, is made up not of water but of oxygen and hydrogen, two gases. The Democritean atomism which we know from Epicurus and Lucretius, however, differs from Daltonian atomism quite as profoundly; for the Greek atoms were indivisible particles of undifferentiated matter, whereas Dalton's atoms (until Rutherford began to split them) were indivisible particles of this or that kind of matter, hydrogen or carbon or lead.

Dalton divided natural substances into two classes: those made up of 'molecules' like water, and those made up of 'atoms', like hydrogen. In each case the particle, molecule or atom, was the smallest quantity of that substance which could exist: but not for the same reason. The molecule of water was the smallest possible amount of water because the only parts into which it could be divided were particles not of water but of oxygen and hydrogen. The atom of oxygen was the smallest possible amount of oxygen not because it was divisible into parts which were not oxygen but because it was not divisible at all.

This conception of a physically indivisible 'atom' was not new. It was a fossilized relic of ancient Greek physics, anachronistically surviving in an alien environment, the evolutionary science of the nineteenth century. The fertile part of Daltonism was not the idea of the 'atom' but the idea of the 'molecule': not the Anaxagorean idea of particles homogeneous with that which they go to make up, but the thoroughly modern idea that particles having determinate special qualities of their own could make up bodies having quite different special qualities. This idea is nowhere to be found in the Greeks. The theory of the 'four elements' in Empedocles is no anticipation of it; for according to that theory the elements earth, air, fire, and water preserve their special qualities in the compounds formed of them, so that these compounds are, as to their own special qualities, in part earthy, in part airy, and so forth.

Indeed, the Daltonian 'atom' did not survive the nineteenth

century. Before that century was over J. J. Thomson and others resolved the Daltonian dualism between the 'atom' and the 'molecule' and brought the theory of the atom into line with the theory of the molecule. This was done by maintaining that, just as the 'molecule' of water was made up of parts which taken separately were not water but something else, namely oxygen and hydrogen, so the 'atom' of oxygen was made up of parts which taken separately were not oxygen but something else, namely, electricity.

(b) *The principle of minimum time.* An evolutionary science of nature will maintain that a natural substance takes time to exist; an appropriate amount of time, different kinds of substance taking each its own specific amount. For each specific substance there is a specific time-lapse during which it can exist; in a shorter time-lapse it cannot exist, because the specific function or process whose occurrence is what we mean when we speak of the specific substance as existing cannot occur in so short a time.

If the suggestion made above was correct, that evolutionary natural science is based on analogy with historical science, and if history is the study of human affairs, human affairs should present us with analogies for this principle, just as they present us with analogies for the principle of minimum space in, for example, the fact that a given type of human activity involves as a minimum a certain number of human beings: that it takes two to make a quarrel, three to make a case of jealousy, four or five (if Plato is right, *Republic*, 369 D) to make a civil society, and so on. And these analogies in human affairs for the principle of minimum time should have been commonplaces long before that principle began to affect the work of natural scientists.

This is in fact the case. A typical and famous example is Aristotle's remark (*Eth. Nic.* 1098ᵃ18) that being happy is an activity which requires a whole lifetime, and cannot exist in less. So, notoriously, with activities like being a strategist or a statesman or a musical composer. Perhaps no one can say exactly how long these take to exist; but one might suggest that to be a strategist requires at least the time of one campaign; to be a statesman, the time of framing and enacting one piece of legislation; to be a composer, the time of composing one musical work. Let t be the time taken by any one of these activities.

Then the occurrence of that activity is possible only granted the occurrence of other activities, occupying a time less than t, which in a loose sense of the phrase may be called the 'parts' of which it is composed. Say a man takes a year to write a book; during a certain minute of that year he writes one sentence and in that sense the writing of the book is a whole of which writing each sentence of it is one part. These 'parts' are not homogeneous with each other or with the 'whole'. Each sentence is the solution of a special problem with its own peculiar characteristics; and the book as a whole is the solution of a problem not like any of these.

Elsewhere Aristotle comes near to applying this notion to things in nature. He points out (*Eth. Nic* 1174^{a}20 seqq.) that 'movements' are made up of parts not homogeneous with each other or with the wholes they make up. He gives as examples the building of a temple and walking. He analyses the former example; I will offer an analysis of the latter. When a man walks at three miles an hour, making three steps in every two seconds, during any given hundredth of a second he cannot properly be said to be walking, for walking is a kind of locomotion effected by standing on each foot alternately while swinging the other forward; he is standing on one foot and raising the other from the ground, or moving it forward, or putting it down with his weight behind it, or standing on the toe of one foot and the heel of the other, or the like. How long exactly it takes for the rhythmical action which is called walking to establish itself may be a question difficult or even impossible to answer with certainty; but clearly a hundredth of a second is not enough.

Aristotle's use here of the word 'movement' suggests the famous argument of Zeno the Eleatic. At any given instant, said Zeno, a flying arrow is not in motion; it is at rest, occupying the space equal to itself in which it is situated; so that if time is nothing but a sum of instants the arrow is never in motion at all. Aristotle, in the passage referred to, points out that a determinate kind of motion requires for its occurrence a determinate lapse of time; which leaves the reader free to answer Zeno, if he will, by saying 'How long exactly it takes for an arrow to be in motion I do not know; but some lapse of time is required. Let an instant be defined as any lapse of time shorter than that; then no contradiction is involved between saying that in a given instant the arrow is at rest and that time is made up of instants, and saying that during a longer period of time the arrow moves.'

Aristotle does not say this; nor is there any evidence that he meant to suggest it. All he says is that a movement of a certain determinate kind is made up of movements not of that kind. That movement as such is made up of parts which are not movement at all he would no doubt have denied. The answer to Zeno which, I have said, he leaves his reader free to make would be a good answer only if it were implemented by a physical theory according to which the arrow, even when 'at rest', were conceived as a microcosm of particles all moving so rapidly that the rhythms of their movement could establish themselves in a lapse of time shorter than that which *ex hypothesi* it takes for the arrow to 'be in motion'.

This is in fact how the arrow is conceived in modern physics. Zeno is answered by negating the hypothesis underlying his argument. We must not say that Zeno is 'refuted', because although his argument is easy to understand in itself, there is much doubt among scholars as to what he meant it to prove: what exactly the problem was upon which he was trying to throw light. It is clear, however, that among the terms of the problem was the distinction between an arrow's being 'in motion' when it is shot through the air and its being 'at rest' when it stands in the quiver or lies on the ground. Evolutionary physics denies this distinction. The arrow is made, say, partly of wood and partly of iron. Each of these is composed of minute particles which move incessantly; those of the wood move in one way, those of the iron in another. These particles are themselves composed of particles still more minute, moving again in ways of their own. However far the physicist can push his analysis, he never arrives at particles which are at rest, and never at particles which behave in exactly the same way as that which they compose. Nor does he think of any one of them, at any stage, as behaving in exactly the same way as any other: on the contrary, the 'laws' according to which he thinks of them as moving are, in his own phrase, 'statistical laws', descriptive of their average behaviour in the mass, not of their individual behaviour when taken separately.

According to the principle of minimum space, wherever there is a natural substance s_1 (such as water), there is a smallest possible quantity of it (the molecule of water), anything less than which will be not a piece of that substance but a piece of a different substance (oxygen or hydrogen). According to the principle of minimum time, there is a minimum time t, during which the movements of the (oxygen and hydrogen) atoms within a single molecule (of water) can establish their rhythm and thus constitute that single molecule. In a lapse of time smaller than t, the (oxygen and hydrogen) atoms exist, but the molecule does not exist. There is no s_1; there is only s_2, the class of substance to which oxygen and hydrogen belong.

But the particles of s_2 are themselves made up of smaller moving particles (electrons, nuclei; up to now the complete analysis has not been finally arrived at); and these will be particles not of s_2 but of s_3 (electricity, negative and positive).

The principles of minimum space and minimum time apply once more. There will be a smallest possible quantity of s_2 (the atom of oxygen or of hydrogen), not necessarily the same for all the different kinds of substance included in that class; the smallest possible quantity of s_3 will be very much smaller. There will also be a smallest possible lapse of time t_2 during which the movements of the s_3 particles within a single s_2 particle can establish their rhythm and thus constitute that s_2 particle; a lapse of time not necessarily the same in length for the various kinds of substance included in the s_2 class, but in every case falling within the limits implied by calling it t_2. In a lapse of time smaller than t_2 there are, therefore, no substances belonging to the class s_2; there is only s_3.

If the question is raised, therefore, whether a given thing is an example of s_1, of s_2, or of s_3, the answer depends on the question: In how long a time? If in a time of the order of t_1, it is an example of s_1; if in a time of the order of t_2, it is an example of s_2; if in a time of the order of t_3, it is an example of s_3. Different orders of substance take different orders of time-lapse to exist.

The implications of this principle have been worked out by Professor A. N. Whitehead and summarized in his dictum[1] that 'there is no nature at an instant'. The tendency of all modern

[1] *Nature and Life*, 1934, p. 48.

science of nature is to resolve substance into function. All natural functions are forms of motion, and all motion takes time. At an instant, not the 'instant' of 'instantaneous' photography, which contains a measurable time-lapse, but a mathematical instant containing no time-lapse at all, there can be no motion, and therefore no natural function, and therefore no natural substance.

The principle, it may be observed in passing, opens no door to subjective idealism. One might express it by saying that how the world of nature appears to us depends on how long we take to observe it: that to a person who took a view of it extending over a thousand years it would appear in one way, to a person who took a view of it extending over a thousandth of a second it would appear in a different way, but that each of these is mere appearance, due to the fact that we take exactly so much time to make our observation.

This, though true, would be misleading. The water which in order to exist requires a time of the order of t_1 is just as real as the oxygen and hydrogen atoms composing it, which require a time of the order of t_2; and these are just as real as the electrons and nuclei composing them, which require a still less time. How the natural world appears to us does certainly depend on how long we take to observe it; but that is because when we observe it for a certain length of time we observe the processes which require that length of time in order to occur.

Another dangerous way of stating the principle is by propounding the hypothesis: Suppose all movement in nature were to stop; and asking, What would be left? According to Greek physics, and equally according to the Renaissance ideas which, with special reference to their formulation by Newton, are nowadays known as 'classical physics', what would be left is the corpse of nature, a cold dead world, like a derelict steam-engine. According to modern physics nothing whatever would be left. This is dangerous because the hypothesis according to which nothing would be left is, for modern physics, a nonsense hypothesis: it implies a distinction between substance and function, and their distinction is exactly what modern physics denies.

The principle may, however, be illustrated by means of other hypotheses incapable of practical realization but not in them-

selves nonsensical. Our experimental knowledge of the natural
world is based on our acquaintance with those natural processes
which we can observe experimentally. This acquaintance is
limited downwards in space and time by our inability to observe
any process that occupies less than a certain amount of space
or a certain lapse of time, and upwards by the impossibility of
observing any process that occupies more space or more time
than the range of human vision or the time covered by human
records, or even by the mere inconvenience of observing processes
that take longer than the time during which it is easy for us to
devote our time to watching them. These limits, upper and
lower, of our observations in space and time have been greatly
enlarged by the apparatus of the modern scientist, but they
still exist, and are ultimately imposed on us by our constitution
as animals of a definite size and living at a definite rate.
Animals much larger or much smaller than ourselves, whose
lives ran in a much slower or a much faster rhythm, would
observe processes of a very different kind, and would reach by
these observations a very different idea from our own as to
what the natural world is like.

Thus the new cosmology entails a certain scepticism as to the
validity of any argument which, starting from our own observations, inductively reasons that what we have observed is a fair
sample of nature in its entirety. Such arguments are doubtless
valid in the sense that the processes we observe may be a fair
sample of processes, whether observable or unobservable to
ourselves, having the same order of extension in space or time;
but they cannot tell us anything about processes very much
larger or smaller in space or very much longer or shorter in time.
The natural world which human scientists can study by observation and experiment is an anthropocentric world; it consists
only of those natural processes whose time-phase and space-
range are within the limits of our observation.[1]

[1] 'The second law of thermodynamics is only true because we cannot deal
practically with magnitudes below a certain limit. If our universe were
populated by intelligent bacteria they would have no need of such a law'
(J. W. N. Sullivan, *The Bases of Modern Science*, ch. v). Professor J. B. S.
Haldane ('On Being the Right Size', in *Possible Worlds*, 1927) has pointed out
that the human organism is exactly intermediate in size between the electron
and the spiral nebula, the smallest and largest existing things. This, he
suggests, gives man a privileged position in the world of nature; exactly as
Aristotle argues (*Politics*, 1327^{b}29) that Greece is fitted to govern the world

This scepticism involves no doubt as to the validity of our observational methods within their own proper field. We still inherit the methods of Renaissance science in this point at least: that we hold no theory to be acceptable until it has been confirmed by observation and experiment; and the 'theory' that natural processes have one type of character within one range of magnitude in space and time, and another when their space-range or time-lapse is different, has been amply confirmed in this way. It is one result, and not the least important, of that enlargement of the limits of our observation by means of modern scientific apparatus, that we are able within our limits as thus enlarged to compare the largest-scale with the smallest-scale processes thus revealed to us, and to note their differences from each other and from those with which observation not so aided acquaints us.

In this way it has been discovered that the Newtonian laws of motion hold good for all motions whose velocity is such as to bring them within range of ordinary human experience, but do not for that reason, as Newton supposed, apply to all velocities whatever, but break down in the case of velocities approaching that of light.

Here, once more, it may be useful to notice that what is true of modern physics is a familiar feature of history. If an historian had no means of apprehending events that occupied more than an hour, he could describe the burning down of a house but not the building of a house; the assassination of Caesar but not his conquest of Gaul; the rejection of a picture by the hanging committee of the Royal Academy but not the painting of it; the performance of a symphony but not its composition. If two historians gave each his own answer to the question: 'What kinds of events happen, or can or might happen, in history?' their answers would be extremely different if one habitually thought of an event as something that takes an hour and the other as something that takes ten years; and a third who conceived an event as taking anything up to 1,000 years would give a different answer again.

We can even say to some extent what kind of differences there would be. In general, making things takes longer than

because it μεσεύει κατὰ τοὺς τόπους and its people has a corresponding character; in other words, the right place for a man is in the centre of his own horizon.

destroying them. The shorter our standard time-phase for an historical event, the more our history will consist of destructions, catastrophes, battle, murder, and sudden death. But destruction implies the existence of something to destroy; and as this type of history cannot describe how such a thing came into existence, for the process of its coming into existence was a process too long to be conceived as an event by this type of history, its existence must be presupposed as given, ready-made, miraculously established by some force outside history.

It would be rash for one who is not himself a natural scientist to venture an opinion as to how close the parallel is between what has just been said of history and anything in the science of nature. I have quoted the late Mr. Sullivan's remark that the second law of thermodynamics applies only from the human point of view and would be unnecessary for an intelligent microbe. If the parallel of which I have spoken is at all close, an intelligent organism whose life had a longer time-rhythm than man's might find it not so much unnecessary as untrue.

The natural processes that come most easily within ordinary human observation, it may be, are predominantly of a destructive kind, like the historical events that come most easily within the knowledge of the historian who thinks of an event as something that takes a short time. Like such an historian, the natural scientist, it may be, is led by this fact to think of events in nature as in the main destructive: releases or dissipations of energy stored he knows not how; to think of the natural world as running down like a clock or being shot away like a store of ammunition.

Such a conception of natural process is not an invention of my own; it is one which we actually find stated over and over again in the writings of natural scientists in our own time. It very closely resembles a view of history which everyone knows to be long out of date: the view according to which historical processes are not constructive but merely destructive in character, with its corollary that what these processes destroy is a given, ready-made, miraculously established form of human life, a primitive Golden Age, concerning which all history can tell us is how it has been progressively eroded by the tooth of time.

That view of history, as everyone knows, is an illusion. It is an illusion incidental to what, perhaps, may be called historical myopia: the habit of seeing short-phase historical events and not seeing those whose time-rhythm is longer. That history is a process in which *tout casse, tout lasse, tout passe,* is doubtless true; but it is also a process in which the things that are thus destroyed are brought into existence. Only it is easier to see their destruction than to see their construction, because it does not take so long.

May it not be the same in the world of nature? May it not be the case that the modern picture of a running-down universe, in which energy is by degrees exchanging a non-uniform and arbitrary distribution (that is, a distribution not accounted for by any laws yet known to us, and therefore in effect a given, ready-made, miraculously established distribution, a physicist's Golden Age) for a uniform distribution, according to the second law of thermodynamics, is a picture based on habitual observation of relatively short-phase processes, and one destined to be dismissed as illusory at some future date, when closer attention has been paid to processes whose time-phase is longer? Or even if these long-phase processes should continue to elude human observation, may it not be found necessary to dismiss the same picture as illusory because, according to the principles of evolutionary physics, we shall find ourselves obliged to postulate such processes even though we cannot directly observe them?

PART I
GREEK COSMOLOGY

I

THE IONIANS

§ 1. The Ionian science of nature

THE Ionian philosophers of the seventh and sixth centuries B.C. devoted so much attention to cosmological problems that Aristotle, who is by far our most important authority for the history of early Greek thought, refers to them in a body as φυσιόλογοι, theorists of nature. According to Aristotle, the characteristic of this Ionian cosmology is the fact that whenever its devotees ask the question: 'What is nature?' they at once convert it into the question: 'What are things made of?' or 'What is the original, unchanging substance which underlies all the changes of the natural world with which we are acquainted?'[1]

People who could ask this question must have already settled in their minds a large number of preliminary points; and if a whole school of thinkers, whose work extends over the best part of a century, could agree in asking the same question the preliminary points must have been very firmly settled. I will mention three of them.

1. *That there are 'natural' things*: in other words, that among the things with which we are acquainted some, no doubt, are 'artificial', that is, are the products of 'skill' on the part of human or other animals, but others are 'natural', the contradictory of 'artificial', things that happen or exist of them-

---

[1] Monsieur E. Bréhier (*Histoire de la Philosophie*, Paris, 1928, vol. i, p. 42) says that the question 'What are things made of?' is not Thales' question but Aristotle's question. There is certainly force in his warning that our traditional view of the Ionian physicists through the spectacles of Aristotle places us in danger of ascribing exaggerated importance in the minds of these men to what may in fact have been little more than *obiter dicta*, and thus projecting fourth-century problems back into the sixth century or even the late seventh. Yet Monsieur Bréhier himself says 'Le phénomène fondamental dans cette physique milésienne est bien l'évaporation de l'eau de la mer sous l'influence de la chaleur' (p. 44). In other words, Monsieur Bréhier in spite of his own warning continues to accept Aristotle's view that the fundamental concept of Ionian physics was the concept of transformation.

selves and not because someone has made them or produced them.

2. *That 'natural' things constitute a single 'world of nature'*: in other words, that the things which happen or exist of themselves have in common not only the negative characteristic of not having been produced by 'skill' but certain positive characteristics as well, so that it is possible to make statements about them which apply not merely to certain selected groups of them but to all of them together.

These two points are indispensable presuppositions of any 'science of nature'. The Greeks had worked them out, through what processes of inquiry or reflection we do not know at all, and with what amount of help from Mesopotamians and Egyptians and other non-Greek peoples we know only very slightly, by the seventh century B.C.

3. *That what is common to all 'natural' things is their being made of a single 'substance' or material.* This was the special or peculiar presupposition of Ionian physics; and the school of Miletus may be regarded as a group of thinkers who made it their special business to take this as their 'working hypothesis' and see what could be made of it: asking in particular the question: 'That being so, what can we say about this single substance?' They did not consciously treat it as a 'working hypothesis': it cannot be doubted that they accepted it as an absolute and unquestioned presupposition of all their thinking; but the historian of thought, looking back on their achievement, cannot fail to see that what they really did was to test this idea of a single universal substance and to find it wanting.

(i) *Thales.* Thales, the founder of this school, was born at Miletus between 630 and 620 B.C. and lived until the fall of Sardis in 546/5. He held, as everyone knows, that the universal substance out of which things are made is water. He left behind him no written works, or at any rate none devoted to this subject;[1] and as early as the time of Aristotle tradition was silent as to why he chose water to play this central role in his

---

[1] Diogenes Laertius tells us that according to some authorities Thales left no written works at all, and that others ascribed to him works on the solstices and the equinoxes. Theophrastus attributes to him a work on astronomy for sailors. There is no reason to believe that he wrote on cosmology; the treatise 'on Beginnings' which Galen quotes (*apud* Diels, *Fragmente der Vorsokratiker*, ed. 4, 1922, vol. i, p. 13) was certainly a forgery of much later date. By Aristotle's

system of nature, and how he conceived the process of 'making' things out of it, that is to say, how exactly he thought that a thing made of water, such as a stone or a fish, differed from the water out of which it was made. On the second question we have no light at all. On the first, Aristotle himself has no information, but he has put forward two suggestions which are admittedly guesses. The first is that moisture is necessary for the nourishment of every organism; the second, that every animal's life begins in seminal fluid.[1]

The point to be noticed here is not what Aristotle says but what it presupposes, namely that Thales conceived the world of nature as an organism: in fact, as an animal. This is confirmed by the fragments which have come down to us of Thales' own utterances. According to these fragments, Thales regarded the world (the earth *plus* the heavens, that is to say; what later Greek thinkers called κόσμος, but the Milesians called οὐρανός) as something 'ensouled', ἔμψυχον, a living organism or animal, within which are lesser organisms having souls of their own; so that a single tree or a single stone is, according to him, both a living organism in itself and also a part of the great living organism which is the world. One such organism within the world is the earth; which Thales, we are told, conceived as floating upon an ocean of water. Since he certainly thought of the earth as alive, and certainly thought of it and everything in it as made of water, and probably also thought, as his pupils certainly thought, that everything in nature was constantly passing away and therefore in need of constant renewal or replacement, he may possibly have conceived the earth as grazing, so to speak, on the water in which it floats, thus repairing its own tissues and the tissues of everything in it by taking in water from this ocean and transforming it, by processes akin to respiration and digestion, into the various parts of its own body. We are told, moreover, that he described the

time it was matter for conjecture what his cosmological doctrines were. Tradition reported various alleged utterances: the fourth-century historian of thought had to think what they might have meant.

[1] λαβὼν ἴσως τὴν ὑπόληψιν ταύτην ἐκ τοῦ πάντων ὁρᾶν τὴν τροφὴν ὑγρὰν οὖσαν . . . καὶ διὰ τὸ πάντων τὰ σπέρματα τὴν φύσιν ὑγρὰν ἔχειν (perhaps deriving this view from the observation that everything has wet nutriment . . . and the fact that the seed of everything is of a wet nature): Aristotle, *Metaphysics*, A, 983ᵇ22–7.

world as ποίημα θεοῦ, something made by God. That is to say, the vital processes of this cosmic organism were not conceived by him as self-existent or eternal (for he said that God is 'older' than the world) but as depending for their existence on an agency prior to them and transcending them.[1]

It is evident from these scanty records that the ideas of Thales were enormously remote from the Renaissance conception of the natural world as a cosmic machine made by a divine engineer in order to serve his purposes. He regarded it as a cosmic animal whose movements, therefore, served purposes of its own. This animal lived in the medium out of which it was made, as a cow lives in a meadow. But now the question arose, How did the cow get there? What transformed the undifferentiated water into that mass of differentiated and ensouled water which we call the world? Here the analogy between the world and a cow breaks down. The cosmic cow did not begin its life as a calf. The life of the world-animal does not include anything analogous to reproduction. The world was not born, it was made; made by the only maker that dare frame its fearful symmetry: God.

But what kind of a making was this? It was very unlike that making which Renaissance cosmology attributed to the 'great architect of the universe'. For Renaissance thought, as that phrase indicates, the creative activity of God in its relation to the world of nature is in all points except one a scaled-up version of the activity by which a man builds a house or a machine; the one exception being that God is an architect or engineer who has no need of materials but can make His world out of nothing. If the divine activity of which Thales spoke in

[1] Diogenes Laertius says that Thales regarded the world as 'ensouled' (ἔμψυχον), i.e. as a living organism, and also repeats Aristotle's statement (de Anima, 405ᵃ19) that he ascribed souls to such things as can originate movement, e.g. a loadstone.

That the earth floats 'like a log of wood' on the cosmic water is reported as the alleged ('they say') opinion of Thales by Aristotle, de Caelo, 294ᵃ28.

That 'God is the oldest thing, for he has no beginning', and that 'the world is the fairest thing, for it is of God's making' are among the sayings ascribed to Thales by Diogenes Laertius.

That the earth 'grazes' on water is not a doctrine anywhere expressed in the fragments of Thales or ascribed to him by any ancient writer, but I am not alone in thinking it implied in the recorded fragments and their context. 'Le monde des choses est donc au milieu de l'eau *et s'en nourrit*' (A. Rey, *La Jeunesse de la Science grecque*, Paris, 1933, p. 40: my italics).

his phrase ποίημα θεοῦ is a scaled-up version of any human activity, this human activity is not the activity of an architect or engineer but the activity of a magician. God, in the cosmology of Thales, makes a cosmic animal out of water as magically as Aaron made a snake out of a walking-stick, or as the Arunta in their *inchitiuma* ceremonies make a supply of emus or witchetty grubs.

(ii) *Anaximander*. Anaximander, towards the middle of the sixth century,[1] modified this teaching in certain important ways. He conceived the earth not as a flat raft-like thing floating on the surface of a sea, but as a solid cylindrical body, like the drum of a column in Greek architecture[2], which floated free in a surrounding medium of the undifferentiated stuff from which it was made. This stuff he regarded not as water (for water, after all, is one example of the specific natural substances whose origin the φυσιόλογος sought to explain) but as something which could only be described by the name τὸ ἄπειρον, the Boundless. By that name he meant both that it is infinite in quantity spatially and temporally, extending indefinitely in every direction as well as backward and forward in time; and also that it is indeterminate in quality, lacking e.g. the special characteristics of liquidity no less than that of solidity or gaseousness.[3] He thought that innumerable worlds arose here and there in this uniform medium like eddies or bubbles, of which ours is one. The Boundless he identified with God, as being deathless and imperishable.[4] Some writers tell us that he also conceived the various worlds as themselves gods.[5] This

---

[1] Diogenes Laertius dates his birth about 610/11 B.C., and his death shortly after 547/6.

[2] κυλινδροειδῆ 'cylindrical', says pseudo-Plutarch (*Strom.* 2; *apud* Diels, p. 16, l. 15) using Theophrastus, 'with its height one-third of its diameter'; cf. Hippolytus, *Ref.* i. 6, *apud* Diels, ibid., l. 33. Diogenes Laertius, however, says that Anaximander regarded the earth as spherical, σφαιροειδῆ (Diels, p. 14, l. 5).

[3] ἀόριστον καὶ κατ' εἶδος καὶ κατὰ μέγεθος 'indefinite both in kind and in extent' (Simplicius, *Phys.* 154, 14, *apud* Diels, p. 16, l. 6, using Theophrastus).

[4] καὶ τοῦτο (sc. τὸ ἄπειρον) εἶναι τὸ θεῖον· ἀθάνατον γὰρ καὶ ἀνώλεθρον 'and the Divine, he said, was this (the Boundless); for this was immortal and indestructible' (Aristotle, *Physics*, iii. 203ᵇ12, *apud* Diels, p. 17, l. 34).

[5] 'Α. ἀπεφήνατο τοὺς ἀπείρους οὐρανοὺς θεούς 'A. declared the innumerable worlds to be gods' (Aëtius, i. 17. 12, *apud* Diels, p. 18, l. 30). *A. autem opinio est nativos esse deos longis intervallis orientis occidentisque, eosque innumerabiles esse mundos* 'but A's opinion is that there are gods, which have come into existence by birth, situated in the plane of the earth's equator at wide intervals.

would appear to stand in flagrant contradiction with his own reported doctrine (unless it is only a gloss, perhaps Aristotelian, upon that doctrine) that what entitled the Boundless to be called God was its infinity and eternity, whereas any given world is finite in extent and finite in the duration of its life.

What could have led Anaximander into such a contradiction we can only guess. This at any rate is clear, that his most notorious departure from the cosmology of his master Thales had a reasoned basis and must have led to reasoned consequences. Water could not be the thing out of which everything is made, because water, as wet, has an opposite, namely the dry. Of a pair of opposites each implies the other, and both must have arisen by differentiation out of something originally undifferentiated. The thing out of which everything is made must be, therefore, the undifferentiated. Within this a creative process occurs by which opposites, the hot and the cold, the wet and the dry, are generated and simultaneously segregated. In this way, we are told, Anaximander did in fact argue. We are also told that he regarded the creative process as consisting of rotary movement, which might arise anywhere in the Boundless and thus give rise to a world in any part of it.

This seems to imply that in theology Anaximander reacted against the transcendence of Thales into a doctrine of immanence.[1] Instead of conceiving God as a sort of divine magician making the world by setting up a process of differentiation within the undifferentiated primary matter, he seems to have thought of world-making as a process which this primary matter set going within itself by originating these local vortices.

and that these are innumerable worlds' (Cicero, *de nat. Deorum*, i. 10. 25, *apud* Diels, p. 18, l. 31). That Anaximander conceived these other worlds as lying in the plane of the equator does not appear from any of our authorities except Cicero.

[1] If Thales really said that 'all things are full of gods' (as Aristotle says, *de Anima*, 411ᵃ8) he cannot have thought of the divine nature as merely transcendent relatively to the world. And this would not be surprising; because a theology of pure and rigid transcendence is a thing as hard to find in the history of thought as one of pure and rigid immanence. At most, it can be said that in this or that theology immanence or transcendence is the prevailing tendency.

But it is not quite certain that the saying belongs to Thales and not to Heraclitus; nor, if it does belong to Thales, what he meant by it; for often in Greek literature souls are called gods, and admittedly Thales thought that all natural bodies were ensouled. See Ueberweg, *Gesch. d. Philos.*, ed. 12 (Berlin, 1926), vol. i, pp. 44–5.

A world is thus a thing that makes itself wherever a vortex arises in the Boundless; hence a world is also a world-maker or a god. The *natura naturata* of this world (to anticipate a very much later distinction) is finite in extent and in the duration of its life; but its *natura naturans* is the creative nature of the Boundless and of its rotary movement, and hence eternal and infinite.

Conjecture may perhaps be pushed one stage farther. It is a paradoxical feature of Thales' cosmology, as we have seen, that according to its doctrines a thing like the loadstone must be both an animal to itself and also a part of the animal which is the earth. Paradoxical, because it breaks the analogy. A man or a bird is an organism. The man's hand or the bird's wing is a part of that organism, but not an organism to itself. A man or a bird is a part of a family or a flock or the like, but this family or flock is not an organism, it is a group of organisms. And the earth is not only an organism of organisms, it is an organism which breeds the organisms that arise in it. Relatively to them it is creative, and thus divine. To anticipate once more a later doctrine, it is a 'secondary cause' on which has been bestowed a creativity which is limited in its scope and specialized in its character but is none the less, in its limited and specialized way, divine. If these distinctions can be drawn the contradiction between immanent and transcendent elements in the cosmology of Anaximander disappears.

(iii) *Anaximenes.* Anaximenes (late sixth century B.C.)[1] returned to the flat-earth theory of Thales, but no longer thought of this flat body as floating on the surface of anything. It floated in the surrounding medium, he said, supported by that medium's density.[2] Like all the Ionians, he believed that

---

[1] Diogenes Laertius dates his birth 'about the time of the fall of Sardis' (546/5) and his death in 528/5 (Diels, p. 22). This would make him only 18–20 years old when he died, which is impossible. Eusebius, no doubt correctly, makes the fall of Sardis coincide not with his birth but with his *floruit*, which conventionally stands at the age of 40; implying that he was born about 585.

[2] τὴν δὲ γῆν πλατεῖαν εἶναι ἐπ' ἀέρος ὀχουμένην 'he said the earth was flat and supported by air' (Hippol. *Ref.* i. 7; *apud* Diels, p. 23, l. 19). τὸ πλάτος αἴτιον εἶναι τοῦ μένειν αὐτήν· οὐ γὰρ τέμνειν ἀλλ' ἐπιπωματίζειν τὸν ἀέρα τὸν κάτωθεν 'he says that the reason why the earth stays still is because it is flat; for it does not divide the air beneath it, but presses down on it like a lid' (Aristotle, *de Caelo*, 294ᵇ13; *apud* Diels, p. 25, l. 24).

Anaximander, in one of his most remarkable intuitions, had seen that the

the medium in which it floated was also the stuff of which it is made. Like Anaximander, he conceived this stuff as a three-dimensional volume extending infinitely in every direction round the world;[1] but in spite of Anaximander's example, he did not see the logical necessity of conceiving it as indeterminate in quality. He went back to Thales and identified it with one specific natural substance, differing from Thales only in calling it, not water, but air or vapour, ἀήρ.[2]

Differences between various natural substances were due to the rarefaction of this vapour into fire or its progressive condensation into wind, cloud, water, earth, and stone.[3] The cosmic vapour gave rise eternally to movement within itself, and this movement, which was rotary, differentiated and segregated the various natural substances, the rarefied portions being thrown off to the periphery and forming stars, the condensed ones gathering at the centre of the vortex and forming the earth.

All this is a good deal like Anaximander. He followed Anaximander also in thinking of the primitive substance as divine: rejecting the transcendent magician-god of Thales and substituting an immanent God identical with the world-creative process itself. But it is a new feature in Anaximenes, so far as we know, that this world-god was for him transcendent as well as immanent, though in a somewhat crudely materialistic sense; for, said he, the divine vapour is not only the substance out of which the world is made, it is also the envelope or integument which wraps it round and holds it together, 'as the human soul', he says in one of his surviving fragments, 'wraps round and holds together the human body'.[4]

earth needed no support because there was no reason why it should fall in any one direction rather than in any other, so it stayed still. τὴν γῆν εἶναι μετέωρον ὑπὸ μηδενὸς κρατουμένην, μένουσαν δὲ διὰ τὴν ὁμοίαν πάντων ἀπόστασιν 'the earth, he said, swings free in space and stays still without any support because everything is at an equal distance from it' (Hippol. Ref. i. 6; apud Diels, p. 16, l. 31). Anaximenes was not able to follow his master's lead here, and had to support his earth on something.

[1] τῷ μεγέθει ἄπειρον 'boundless in extent' (pseudo-Plutarch, Strom. 3; apud Diels, p. 23, l. 2).

[2] In Homer and Hesiod ἀήρ means 'mist' or 'haze'.

[3] διαφέρειν δὲ μανότητι καὶ πυκνότητι κατὰ τὰς οὐσίας, καὶ ἀραιούμενον μὲν πῦρ γίνεσθαι κ.τ.λ. 'it differs in rarity or density, he says, according to the differences between substances; rarefied, it becomes fire, etc.' (Simplicius, Phys., 24. 26; derived from Theophrastus; apud Diels, p. 22, l. 18).

[4] οἷον ἡ ψυχή, φησίν, ἡ ἡμετέρα ἀὴρ οὖσα συγκρατεῖ ἡμᾶς, καὶ ὅλον τὸν κόσμον

Like Anaximander, again, Anaximenes believed in a plurality of worlds; and like Anaximander (and doubtless for the same reasons) he appears to have called each of them a god. But apparently these worlds were not, like Anaximander's, outside one another in space, but outside one another in time, one perishing and another arising. At any given time, he seems to have thought, there could be no more than one.[1]

By comparison with the shadowy but gigantic figure of Thales and the equally great and far more plainly discernible Anaximander, Anaximenes is neither very impressive nor very interesting. Most of what we know about his ideas is simply a repetition of Anaximander. Where he differs from Anaximander he differs almost uniformly for the worse. We are told of no more than one single idea in his cosmology which appears to have been genuinely original and was to prove fertile; and even this did not prove fertile in his own hands, because the possibilities of progress which it contained could be actualized only by someone who was willing for their sake to abandon the first principles of Ionian cosmology and launch out on a new path.

This idea was the idea of condensation and rarefaction. Anaximander had grappled with the question: 'Why, if the various kinds of natural substances are all made of the same original matter, do they behave in different ways?' He had answered: 'Because opposites are differentiated and segregated out of the original undifferentiated matter by its rotary movement.' But we have no reason to believe that Anaximander was able to show any cause why movement in an undifferentiated matter should generate within it the opposites of which he spoke, namely hot and cold, wet and dry.

Anaximenes, it is clear, was conscious of this defect in his

πνεῦμα καὶ ἀὴρ περιέχει 'just as according to Anaximenes our soul, which is air, holds us together, so the world as a whole is enveloped in its breath, that is, air' (Aëtius, i. 3. 4; *apud* Diels, p. 26, l. 20).

[1] γενητὸν δὲ καὶ φθαρτὸν τὸν ἕνα κόσμον ποιοῦσιν ὅσοι ἀεὶ μέν φασιν εἶναι κόσμον, οὐ μὴν τὸν αὐτὸν ἀεί, ἀλλὰ ἄλλοτε ἄλλον γινόμενον κατά τινας χρόνων περιόδους, ὡς 'Αναξιμένης 'those who like Anaximenes say that there is always a world, but not the same world for ever, because from time to time a fresh one comes into existence after a certain lapse of time, regard the one world as subject to coming into existence and passing away' (Simplicius, *Phys.*, 1121. 12; *apud* Diels, p. 24, l. 20). *Nec deos negavit nec tacuit; non tamen ab ipsis aërem factum, sed ipsos ex aëre ortos credidit* 'he neither denied the gods nor passed them over in silence, but he held not that the air was made by them but that they had arisen from the air' (Augustine, *de civ. Dei*, viii. 2; *apud* Diels, p. 24, l. 16).

master's cosmology and tried to remove it. How does it happen, he asked, that a man can blow hot and cold? It all depends, he answered in the longest of his surviving fragments, on whether you blow with your mouth wide open or nearly shut. Open your mouth wide when you blow, and your breath will come out warm. Blow with your lips close together, and it comes out cold. What is the difference between the two cases? Only this: that when you blow with your mouth wide open the air comes out at low pressure, whereas when you blow with your lips nearly closed the air is compressed.[1]

Here, then, is an experiment of the utmost importance for cosmology. In the first place, we have a substance, air, assuming opposite qualities (hot and cold) under the influence of motion, as Anaximander said. Thus, on this crucial point, Anaximander was right. Secondly, we can make good the defect in Anaximander's statement by providing what Aristotle was to call a 'middle term' between motion on the one hand and the opposites hot-cold on the other. The middle term is condensation-rarefaction. When motion condenses air, cold is generated; when it rarefies it, heat.

It would not be surprising to learn that this was what induced Anaximenes to give up the indeterminate primary matter of Anaximander and identify the primary matter with air. An indeterminate primary matter, one might fancy him arguing, is a mere nothing about which nothing can be discovered and nothing said. Part, at least, of what Anaximander wanted to say about his indeterminate primary matter can really be said, and not only said but proved, about air.

Here Anaximenes was making progress. He was going beyond his master Anaximander by making good, as I have said, a defect in Anaximander's statement as to how movement in the primary substance generates opposites in it. But in making this progress he was leaving the world of Ionian physics behind him and pointing the way towards another, as yet non-

---

[1] ὅθεν οὐκ ἀπεικότως λέγεσθαι τὸ καὶ θερμὰ τὸν ἄνθρωπον ἐκ τοῦ στόματος καὶ ψυχρὰ μεθιέναι· ψύχεται γὰρ ἡ πνοὴ πιεσθεῖσα καὶ πυκνωθεῖσα τοῖς χείλεσιν, ἀνειμένου δὲ τοῦ στόματος ἐκπίπτουσα γίγνεται θερμὸν ὑπὸ μανότητος 'and so, says Anaximenes, there is nothing unreasonable in the saying that a man blows both hot and cold. For breath is chilled through compression and condensation by the lips; but when it issues easily through a relaxed mouth it comes warm, owing to rarefaction' (Plutarch, de prim. frig., 7. 947 seqq.; apud Diels, p. 26, ll. 9–13).

existent, type of physical science. He had broken the rules of
physics, as the game of physics was played in his time. He had
earned for himself an epitaph like the inscription in Rugby
School close which commemorates William Webb Ellis, 'who
with a fine disregard of the rules of Rugby football as played
in his time first picked up the ball and ran with it, thus creating
the modern Rugby game'. Thus from the point of view of the
Ionian School, to which he is conventionally assigned, Anaximenes is an example of decadence. From another point of view
he is not an example of decadence but an example of progress;
and from this point of view he does not belong to the Ionian
school, he is the link between it and the Pythagorean.

This statement must be documented both negatively and
positively: negatively by showing that Anaximenes was no
longer a true Ionian; positively by showing that he had already
embarked on the Pythagorean enterprise.

That he was not a true Ionian is clear from two facts: first,
that he went back on the quite conclusive demonstration by
which Anaximander had shown that a really primitive universal
substance must be indeterminate in quality and could therefore no more be identified with air than it could with water;
secondly, that his main interest seems to have swung away
from the oneness of the primitive substance to the manyness of
the various natural substances, each with its own proper mode
of behaviour. Anaximenes, if I interpret him correctly, had
lost interest in the question: 'What is the one thing out of
which all things are made?' This, according to Aristotle, was
the central question of Thales and his school. In so far as
Anaximenes had lost interest in it he had ceased to be a
member of that school. Anaximander had reduced the question
to absurdity, and Anaximenes left it there.

That he was a nascent Pythagorean is clear from his insistence on the concept of condensation and rarefaction. His
question was: 'Why do different kinds of things behave differently?' That is not the question of Ionian physics, it is the
question of Pythagorean physics. His answer was: 'Because
the thing out of which they are made, no matter what that
thing is, undergoes different arrangements in space.' That is
the Pythagorean answer. As put forward by Anaximenes
it was only a bare rudiment of Pythagoreanism. The only

difference of arrangement of which Anaximenes spoke was the difference between a denser and a looser packing of matter in space. Pythagoreanism was to go much farther than this. But even this is an appeal from the conception of substance to the conception of arrangement, from the conception of matter to the conception of form; and that is why Anaximenes, though he has never been represented in that light by any historian of philosophy,[1] ought to be called not so much a member of the Ionian school as a link between that and the school of Pythagoras.

§ 2. *Limits of Ionian natural science*

The Ionians agreed in conceiving the world as a local differentiation in a homogeneous primitive matter. What the world is made of is, they thought, identical with what it is surrounded by. Thales appears to have distinguished this primitive matter from God, but his successors identified the two, conceiving the undifferentiated primitive matter as creating within itself the differentiations which are worlds.

Neither alternative is satisfactory. If you begin your cosmology by postulating a uniform matter, and go on to say that the world is a local differentiation in this matter, you are logically obliged to give some reason why the differentiation should have occurred where it did occur rather than somewhere else. But by defining the original matter as uniform you have precluded yourself from giving any such reason, or even from leaving a loophole for future discovery by saying that there must have been some reason although you do not know what it was.

You cannot now solve the problem by saying that God chose to create the world at a certain place chosen by Himself in the uniform matter. This is presumably what Thales said: but it is not sense. Unless God had a reason for His choice, it was no choice; it was something of which we have no conception

---

[1] Monsieur A. Rey nearly sees it: *La Jeunesse de la Science grecque*, Paris, 1933, p. 94: 'Car le procès de raréfaction et de condensation n'est plus une métamorphose qualitative. Il est bien une transformation d'ordre quantitatif destinée à rendre intelligible la transformation qualitative elle-même. . . . Voilà déjà le pressentiment' (the reader expects to see 'du Pythagorisme', but Monsieur Rey, like a true Frenchman, jumps to the seventeenth century) 'du morceau de cire de Descartes.'

whatever, and calling it a choice is merely throwing dust in our own eyes by pretending to equate it with a familiar human activity, the activity of choosing, which we do not in fact conceive it to have resembled. Choice is choice between alternatives, and these alternatives must be distinguishable, or they are not alternatives; moreover, one must in some way present itself as more attractive than the other, or it cannot be chosen.

Nor is the problem solved by saying that the primitive matter, being capable of setting itself in motion, was its own God and chose the place within itself at which the differentiation was to be produced. This is presumably what Anaximander and Anaximenes said. Whether God is immanent or transcendent the dilemma is the same. To speak of Him as choosing implies either that He chooses for a reason, in which case the alternatives between which He chooses are already differentiated and the uniformity of the original matter is abandoned; or else He chooses for no reasons, in which case He does not choose.

And the dilemma cannot be evaded by a profession of reverent ignorance. You cannot wriggle out of it by saying that these are mysteries into which you will not pry; that God's ways are past finding out, or (if you prefer one kind of humbug to another) that these are ultimate problems, or, if you like, metaphysical problems which wise men know are insoluble and which we should be content to look squarely in the face and pass on. To do them justice, the Ionians attempted no such evasion. Humbug of that kind arises from a sort of pseudo-religiosity which was not among the vices of the Greek mind. It is humbug, because it was yourself that began prying into these mysteries. You dragged the name of God into your cosmology because you thought you could conjure with it. You now find you cannot; which proves, not that God is great, but that you are a bad conjurer.

In other words: the dilemma does not arise out of the nature of things, it arises out of the way in which Ionian natural science tried to deal with its own problems. The moral was, not that the nature of things was inscrutable, but that Ionian natural science had made a false move; in particular, that it was a false move to assume that a cosmology could be built upon a materialistic foundation. You can argue backwards, if that is what you want to do, from the world of natural things to the idea of a primitive universal matter or substance out of which it is made; but there are two limitations from which no project of this kind can ever escape.

1. You must not hope, as the Ionians hoped, for a clear mental picture of this substance. You construct the idea by a process of abstraction in which all the differences between different kinds of natural substances are omitted; what is left when that process is complete will certainly not be, as Thales imagined, water; it will certainly not be, as Anaximenes fancied, air; Anaximander found the right answer when he described it as the indefinite or indeterminate.

2. You must not hope, as the Ionians hoped, to reverse the process. Granted that it is possible, by leaving out all the differences between different kinds of natural substances, to arrive at an abstract idea of a single universal primitive matter, you cannot then argue forwards again from this primitive matter to the world of nature as we know it. From a uniform primitive matter to a natural world made out of it there is no logical passage.

Because the Ionians overlooked these two impossibilities, and staked everything on the hope of (1) describing in a concrete manner the universal primitive substance, and (2) explaining how the world of nature as known to us has been made out of it, the first great enterprise of European natural science ended in failure. The history of science, in so far as it is a history of scientific progress, consists not so much in the progressive accumulation of facts as in the progressive clarification of problems. What makes a natural scientist is not his knowledge of facts about nature but his ability to ask questions about nature: first, to ask questions at all, instead of merely waiting to see what turns up; and secondly, to ask intelligent questions, that is, answerable questions: intrinsically answerable questions, as distinct from nonsensical questions, and questions answerable relatively to the information at his disposal, as distinct from questions that would be answerable only if he had access to facts which are hidden from him. No doubt, the Ionian physicists asked innumerable questions which were in both these senses answerable, and many of these, no doubt, they answered correctly. At any rate, there can be no doubt on either of these points in the mind of any one capable of appreciating the enormous intellectual energy that is attested by their surviving fragments. But the general plan of their natural science was vitiated, not by the fact of their being confined to naked-eye observations unaided by the instruments of the modern laboratory, but by the fact of their standing committed to the asking of two questions which, because they were nonsense questions, no refinement of laboratory technique would have enabled them to answer:

(1) How can we form a clear mental picture of the universal primitive substance?

(2) How, from this primitive substance, can we deduce the world of nature?

§ 3. *Meaning of the word 'nature'*

I said that the Ionian physicists, when they asked the question 'What is nature?', at once converted it into the question 'What are things made of?' Before we leave the Ionians I must add a comment on this remark. It may seem that the Ionian physicists' minds were working at this point a little oddly. A modern European, if he were asked the same question, 'What is nature?' would be likelier to turn it into the question 'What kinds of things exist in the natural world?' and to answer it by embarking on a descriptive account of the natural world, or natural history.

This is because in modern European languages the word 'nature' is on the whole most often used in a collective sense for the sum total or aggregate of natural things. At the same time, this is not the only sense in which the word is commonly used in modern languages. There is another sense, which we recognize to be its original and, strictly, its proper sense: when it refers not to a collection but to a 'principle', again in the proper sense of that word, a *principium*, ἀρχή, or source. We say that the nature of ash is to be pliant, the nature of oak to be tough. We say that a man has a quarrelsome or affectionate nature. We say, 'Let dogs delight to bark and bite ... for 'tis their nature too'. Here the word 'nature' refers to something which makes its possessor behave as it does; this source of its behaviour being something within itself: had it been outside it, the behaviour proceeding from it would have been, not 'natural', but due to 'constraint'. If a man walks fast because he is strong and energetic and determined, we say that fast walking is natural to him. If he walks as fast because a big dog is pulling him along by a lead, we say that his fast walking is due not to his nature but to constraint or compulsion.

The word φύσις is used in Greek in both these ways; and there is the same relation between the two senses in Greek as there is between the two senses in English. In our earlier documents of Greek literature, φύσις always bears the sense which we recognize as the original sense of the English word 'nature'. It always means something within, or intimately belonging to, a thing, which is the source of its behaviour. This is the only sense it ever bears in the earlier Greek authors, and remains throughout the history of Greek literature its normal sense. But very rarely, and relatively late, it also bears the secondary sense of the sum total or aggregate of natural things, that is, it becomes more or less synonymous with the word κόσμος, 'the world'. For example Gorgias,[1] the famous Sicilian of the late fifth century, wrote a book called Περὶ τοῦ μὴ ὄντος, ἢ περὶ φύσεως: and from what ancient writers tell us about the contents of this book it is clear that the word φύσις in its title meant not a principle but an aggregate: not that in things which makes them behave as they do, but the world of nature.

By the Ionian philosophers, I take it, φύσις was never used in this secondary sense, but always in its primary sense. 'Nature', for them, never meant the world or the things which go to make up the world, but always something inhering in these things which made them behave as they did. So the question 'What is nature?' as addressed to an early Ionian philosopher could not possibly suggest to him the compilation of a 'natural history', a compendious description of natural objects and natural facts, and such a philosopher, if he published a book under the title 'on nature', περὶ φύσεως, could not possibly have intended by

[1] He lived, apparently, from early in the fifth century until early in the fourth: roughly, perhaps, 483–375 (so Ueberweg, Gesch. d. Philos., ed. 12, Berlin, 1926, vol. i, p. 120). For testimonia, see Diels, No. 76, vol. ii, pp. 235–66. From these it appears that Gorgias argued (1) that nothing exists; (2) that if anything did exist it could not be known; (3) that if anyone did know something to exist he could not impart his knowledge. It is clear from this what he meant by φύσις.

using that title to convey to his readers that natural objects or natural facts were what he meant to describe in the book. A book so entitled, at that period in the history of Greek literature, would be not a natural history or account of what things there are in the world of nature, but an explanatory science of nature, an account of the principle in virtue of which things in the world of nature behave as they do.

This is a merely lexicographical statement as to what the word φύσις means in all the earlier documents of Greek literature, and in most of the later ones as well. The other senses which the word bears in Greek are all either reducible to it or capable of being explained as derived from it ; and anyone who wants authority for it may be referred to the long and elaborate treatment of the word in Aristotle's dictionary of philosophical terms,[1] which I shall have to discuss more fully in another place (see pp. 80 ff.).

The original and proper meaning of φύσις in Greek, as I have said, is the same as the original and proper meaning of 'nature' in English: and for the very good reason that the English word is really nothing but the Latin translation of the Greek. For example, a bullet flies through the air because the powder behind it has exploded. We should not say that it flies 'by nature', because the explosion was not in the bullet; the momentum it conveyed to the bullet was conveyed to the bullet from outside, and therefore the flight of the bullet is not 'natural' behaviour in the bullet but behaviour under constraint. But if in its flight the bullet penetrates a plank, it does so because it is heavy enough to go through it instead of being stopped by it, as a lighter missile would have been even though travelling at the same velocity; therefore its penetrating power, so far as that is a function of its weight, is a function of its 'nature', and to that extent penetrating the plank is 'natural' behaviour on the part of the bullet.

This is how the Ionians used the word 'nature', exactly as we sometimes use it still. Such use of a word does not commit the user to any scientific or philosophical theory. If the word 'nature' means the internal source of a thing's behaviour, a person who uses the word does not thereby commit himself to the assertion that anything signified by it actually exists. A

[1] *Metaphysics, Δ*, 1014ᵇ16–1015ᵃ19.

man might say that there was no such thing as 'nature', meaning by this not, as Gorgias meant, that there is no world of existing things, but that there is no internal source from which the behaviour of things proceeds. He might say that every detail in the behaviour of everything was due to a special *ad hoc* act of will on the part of an omnipotent God. In that case the word 'nature' would still be used in its original sense, but the existence of any such thing would be denied.

Still less does the use of the word 'nature' commit the user to any theory as to whether the different things that exist in the world have different natures or one and the same nature. 'Is nature one or many?' is a question upon which the mere fact that the word 'nature' is used throws no light whatever. A person who uses the word is, so far as that goes, equally at liberty to say that there is one 'nature' or that there are many 'natures', with no upward or downward limit to the question 'How many?' It will, of course, be understood that the question 'Is nature one or many?' does not mean 'Is the natural world one collection of things or many such collections?' That is a question which a sensible man would not trouble to ask. It means 'Do the various kinds of behaviour which we find in the world proceed from one principle or from a number of different principles?'

Least of all does mere use of the word 'nature' commit the user to any theory as to what in itself the thing is which, in relation to the behaviour of the things that have it, is called their 'nature'. For 'nature', in what I have called its original sense, is a relative term. A thing's 'nature' is the thing in it which makes it behave as it does. When this is said, the question still remains perfectly open, 'What is the thing in it which makes it behave as it does?' To say 'Its nature' does not answer the question, because to say 'Its nature is what makes it behave as it does' is to utter a tautology and therefore to give no information. It is like answering the question 'Who is that lady married to?' by saying 'Her husband'.

On all these three points the Ionian philosophers did in fact hold definite views. They believed that there was such a thing as 'nature'; they believed that nature was 'one'; and they believed that the thing which in its relation to behaviour was called nature was in itself substance or matter. But these were philosophical or scientific doctrines; and they might have abandoned any one of them without abandoning their use of the word 'nature', or modified any of them without modifying the sense in which they used it. For example, someone might have said that the internal cause of a thing's behaviour is not what it is made of, but the arrangements of its parts: not its 'matter' but its 'form'. In that case he might have said: 'The true nature of things is not matter but form.' This would not imply a change in the meaning attached to the word 'nature'. All that has altered is its application.

The point has to be cleared up because it has been left in a state of confusion in the works of a very distinguished scholar, John Burnet, to whom all students of early Greek philosophy look as to one of their most valuable guides. Burnet says that the word φύσις 'meant originally the particular stuff of which a given thing is made. For instance, wooden things have one φύσις, rocks another, flesh and blood a third. The Milesians asked for the φύσις of all things' (*Greek Philosophy, Thales to Plato*, London, 1920, p. 27). This is like saying that for Mrs. Doe 'husband' means John Doe, whereas for Mrs. Roe it means Richard Roe. True, but misleading. Mrs. Doe and Mrs. Roe are agreed as to what it is that makes a man a husband; they are agreed that it is a peculiar relation between him and a certain woman. In the first instance each of them is chiefly interested in one example of this relation, namely the example that involves herself; so when Mrs. Doe calls 'husband' she means to call John, and when Mrs. Roe calls 'husband' she means to call Richard. This is not because they use the word 'husband' in different senses; it is because they are married to different men. So, when Burnet says 'the Milesians believed that what appears in these three forms' (solid, liquid, and gaseous) 'was one thing, and this, as I hold, they called φύσις' (ibid.), what he says is quite true, but it is misleading, and in fact it has even misled himself. He thinks he has detected a peculiar and 'original' meaning of the word φύσις. This is an illusion. He has only detected a case in which that word was applied to a peculiar thing, namely the universal primitive substance, for a peculiar reason, namely that this was held to be the internal source of all such behaviour as had an internal source; just as Mrs. Doe applied the word 'husband' to a peculiar man, namely a tall, thin, clean-shaven one, for a peculiar reason, namely that she was married to him.

The point Burnet is discussing is not a point about the sense of the word φύσις, as he thinks it is, but a point about the discovery of something to which it was thought that the word could be correctly, and in its ordinary sense, applied. The Ionians, as Burnet rightly says, applied the word to that out of which everything was made. In order to be thus applied, the word must have already had a meaning, established in spoken or written usage; just as, if Mrs. Doe says 'John is my husband', the word 'husband', as she uses it, must already have a meaning of its own, and cannot be merely an alternative name for John. What the word φύσις meant in early Greek, Burnet does not seem to have asked; he has only asked to what things it was, by various persons, applied.

II

THE PYTHAGOREANS

§ 1. *Pythagoras*

PYTHAGORAS is one of the most important figures in the history of Greek thought. He is also one of the most shadowy. Our ancient authorities give us one dated event in his biography, and only one: namely, that he left Samos his birthplace and migrated to southern Italy because he objected to the rule of the tyrant Polycrates, which began in 532. We are also told that he settled on the Calabrian coast, at Croton, and there founded a community with a strictly defined rule of life and a function partly religious, partly philosophical and scientific, and partly political. On the assumption that he would not have left Samos for such a cause before he was old enough to know his own mind, ancient writers assume that when Polycrates became tyrant Pythagoras had attained that intellectual maturity which they call ἀκμή and place somewhat arbitrarily at the age of 40. This would date the birth of Pythagoras about 572, but that is the merest guess. He is said to have died about 497, but that is obviously a second guess, based on the assumption that he lived to the age of 75.

The Pythagorean community at Croton had a stormy history and was finally dissolved after the middle of the fifth century. Survivors scattered and kept the Pythagorean tradition alive in various parts of the Greek world; but none of them appears to have put it down in writing, and Pythagoras himself had written nothing; accordingly, when Aristotle came to write the history of Greek thought, he found himself unable to distinguish the ideas of Pythagoras from those of his followers, and equally unable to distinguish the ideas of his early followers from those of Pythagoreans living at a much later date. To-day, in spite of hard work by many generations of scholars, 'Pythagoreanism' is little more than the name of a fluctuating and shapeless body of doctrine, some parts of which can be traced back as far as the fifth century B.C., others as far as the fourth, others not farther than the early centuries A.D.

We are here concerned only with the cosmological element in

this body of doctrine; and I shall try to put together a rough sketch, altogether inferential and quite unsupported by ancient authority except at very few points, of the way in which Pythagoras himself may have dealt with the problem of nature.

Passing his youth at Samos, Pythagoras presumably grew up in the scientific atmosphere of Ionia. He must have been born before Thales died, and his youth at Samos fell partly, perhaps, within the lifetime of Anaximander and wholly within that of Anaximenes. In any case, the doctrines of the Ionian school long survived its founders and were still being taught in the fifth century; so that even if Pythagoras was never a pupil of the three early masters of the school, it does not follow that he owed nothing to them. In fact, from what we know of Pythagoreanism, it must have been founded by a man deeply versed in Ionian natural science, a man whose whole intellectual life had been conditioned by it, in part positively and in part negatively: a man who at certain points accepted and perpetuated its teaching, and at certain other points decisively criticized it.

The Pythagorean cosmography, or picture of the world, suggests that Pythagoras in this respect remained a true disciple of the Ionian school. Like Anaximenes, he pictured the world as suspended in a boundless three-dimensional ocean of vapour and inhaling nourishment from it. Like both Anaximenes and Anaximander, he thought of it as a rotating nucleus in this vapour, having the earth at its centre; the rotary movement serving to generate and segregate opposites. A new discovery of his own seems to have been that the earth is spherical in shape.

In his cosmology or theoretical commentary on this picture Pythagoras broke new ground, with momentous consequences. So definite was the breach on this point between Pythagoras and his predecessors that we can guess with some certainty how his thought actually moved.

He must have seen that in their conception of primary matter the Ionians were on the horns of a dilemma. If they tried to give any definite account of it, e.g. by making up their minds whether it was water or vapour or the like, they were asking a question that could have no answer: not because we do not happen to know which alternative is the right one, but because any alternative is fatal to the theory as a whole. If the primary matter is really that out of which all things are made, it cannot be any more like one of the things that can be made out of it than another: no more like water than mist or fire or earth. It must in fact be wholly devoid of intrinsic character (as indeed Anaximander had already seen); and when one tried to say something about it in positive as opposed to negative terms, the most one could say about it was that it occupied space.

But if the Ionians took this other alternative, of maintaining that the primary matter has no intrinsic character, they were impaled on the other horn of the dilemma. On this alternative it would have to be maintained, as it was by Anaximenes the immediate master of Pythagoras, that the primary matter became fire, mist, water, or earth by being rarefied or condensed. But this rarefaction and condensation implied a distinction between the matter itself and the space it occupied; for it implied that varying amounts of matter might be got into the same space, and the same amount of matter might occupy more space or less. But if matter is wholly indeterminate or devoid of specific character, how can it be distinguished from the space it occupies? For a cubic foot of it is a cubic foot of nothing in particular, and there is no way of distinguishing this from a cubic foot of empty space. Working along this line one gets to a *reductio ad absurdum* of the Ionic cosmology: the conception of matter cannot be distinguished from the conception of void, and the whole edifice of theory falls to the ground.

But Pythagoras was not content to leave the question here. His Ionian predecessors had already made considerable progress with geometry, and he himself had brilliant gifts for the same science. He found that there was a possible connexion, hitherto overlooked, between the problems of cosmology and the achievements of geometry. Different geometrical figures have qualitative differences, although, being all alike merely spatial shapes, they have no material peculiarities, only formal ones. Building on this new foundation, Pythagoras suggested that the qualitative differences in nature were based on differences of geometrical structure. This at any rate was the doctrine of the Pythagorean school, and we can hardly be wrong in attributing it to Pythagoras himself. The point of the new theory is that we need not henceforward bother to ask what the primitive matter is like; that makes no difference; we need not ascribe to it any character differing from that of space itself: all we *must* ascribe to it is the power of being shaped geometrically. The nature of things, that by virtue of which they severally and collectively are what they are, is geometrical structure or form.

This was a great advance on the Ionian theory. The Ionians had been unable to explain differences between different kinds of things. These differences could not be grounded in matter, because matter was homogeneous and undifferentiated; and not only have they in any case to be regarded as non-natural and imposed from without, arbitrarily, but even this imposition from without is impossible if, as seems to be the case, the condensation and rarefaction of matter is impossible. For Thales, an active magnet and an active worm are both of them water and nothing but water. Why then does one of them behave like a magnet and the other like a worm? A theory of the Ionian type can give no answer: it has in fact to deny that there is such a thing as magnet-nature or worm-nature, that is, to deny that the characteristic behaviour of a magnet or worm is natural to it. But suppose that a magnet was a magnet and a worm a worm because of their respective geometrical structures; and suppose that the nature of things meant nothing but this geometrical structure: then each type of behaviour would be natural to that kind of thing. Thus in principle Pythagoras made it possible to answer the questions which the Ionians found unanswerable; and in practice he actually did give valid and well-established answers to questions of this type.

The field in which he achieved this success was that of acoustics. He showed that the qualitative differences between one musical note and another depend not on the material of which the strings producing these notes are made but solely on their rates of vibration: that is to say, on the way in which any given string successively, in a regular rhythm, takes up a determinate series of geometrical shapes. Alter the tempo of this rhythm and you alter the note; produce the same rhythm in two different strings, and you make them both yield the same note. Moreover, he showed that there was a significant relation between the quality of 'concordance' in musical intervals[1] and

<hr>

[1] The words 'concordant' and 'discordant', in Greek music, refer not to

the mathematical simplicity of the corresponding ratios. The ratios $1:2$, $2:3$, $3:4$, yield 'concordant' intervals; further ratios in the same series become progressively 'discordant', though each of them has a unique quality of its own. Thus Pythagoras found it possible to produce a theory of music in mathematical terms: not merely an acoustical theory, accounting for differences of pitch, but an aesthetic theory, accounting for the difference between concord and discord. The 'nature' of musical sounds, their acoustical nature and their aesthetic nature alike, was accounted for by working out the consequences of the assumption that a thing's 'nature'—that in it which makes it behave as it does—is not what it is made of but its structure, as that structure can be described in mathematical terms.

The great triumph of Pythagoreanism in its own lifetime lay here, in the region of musical theory; but it was recognized from the first that this was only an earnest of other triumphs to come. If a musical instrument could be regarded as a rhythmical complex of geometrical shapes, why not a magnet or a worm? And the history of science shows that in principle Pythagoras was right. When chemistry correlates the qualitative peculiarities of water with the formula H_2O, this is a further application of the Pythagorean principle; and the whole of modern physics, with its mathematical theories of light, radiation, atomic structure, and so forth, is a continuation of the same line of thought and a vindication of the Pythagorean point of view. When a modern scientist says that he does not know whether light is made of corpuscles or waves, and that he thinks of it sometimes in one way and sometimes in the other, but that he knows a great deal about its velocity, refraction, and so forth, all of which knowledge can be expressed in equations, he is echoing what we may imagine Pythagoras to have told his disciples: that it makes no difference what the world is made of, and that what we have to study is the patterns and changes of pattern which this primitive matter, whatever it may be, adopts and undergoes.

The spectacular success of the Pythagorean revolution in

combinations of notes in harmony but to successions of notes in melody; though in harmony, when harmony was invented, similar rules were found to hold good.

natural science is not difficult to understand, if one remembers wherein that revolution consisted. It consisted in giving up the attempt to explain the behaviour of things by reference to the matter or substance out of which they were made, and trying instead to explain their behaviour by reference to their form, that is, their structure regarded as something of which a mathematical account could be given. The reason why this change of attitude was so successful was that in order to explain the behaviour of things it was necessary to do justice both to resemblances between the behaviours of different things and to differences between them. The attempt to explain such behaviour in terms of matter could not satisfy both these demands. If you stop short of one single ultimate primitive matter, you have left your task only half-done. If you push it to a conclusion and reach one single ultimate primitive matter, you have flattened out all the differences. Matter, regarded as a principle, is either too uniform or not uniform enough. But mathematical form is a principle which differentiates itself into a hierarchy of mathematical forms, infinitely infinite in their variety: the triangle, the square, the pentagon . . . ; the pyramid, the cube, the dodecahedron . . . ; the ratios $1 : 2, 2 : 3, 3 : 4 \ldots$; and so on *ad infinitum*. Since this series of series of forms contains within itself the ground of its own differentiation, it provides a possible explanation for the differences between innumerable kinds of things.

There was a second reason, at once more interesting topically and more profound philosophically, for the success of Pythagoreanism. The Ionians had been working simultaneously at physics and mathematics. It does not appear that in their own minds the two had ever come into effective contact. Their physics had broken down because it had appealed to a principle, namely abstract matter, which was unknowable and unintelligible. The Pythagoreans, or Pythagoras himself (for whoever did a thing so simple was a genius of the first order), pointed out that the Ionians had been making a lock during one part of their working time and a key to fit it during the rest. What the problem of physics needed for its solution was to be approached from the standpoint of mathematics. The principle of which physics stood in need, hitherto vainly identified with something unintelligible, namely matter, was now identified with something supremely intelligible, namely mathematical truth. Once people had learned how to think mathematically (and the Greeks had learned that from the Ionians) it was obvious that mathematics provided a field in which the human mind was completely at home: a field in which clear and certain knowledge was more attainable than in any other: far more so than in the astronomical predictions or cosmological specula- tions of Ionia. This peculiarly clear and certain kind of know- ledge was put by the Pythagoreans (perhaps we ought to say, was put by Pythagoras) in a quite new but instantaneously convincing position on the map, as knowledge of the essence of things; not only of shapes which things may assume but of what gives them their peculiar properties and their differences from one another. Incidentally this gave a most powerful stimulus to mathematical studies; but its philosophical impor- tance was still greater, as a declaration that the essence of things, what makes them what they are, is supremely intelligible.

Hence, when Socrates claimed that ethical concepts were even more intelligible than mathematical, and when he or his pupil Plato identified the ultimate nature of things with the concept of the good, the new movement of thought, though to some extent it diverted attention from mathematics, was philo- sophically no change at all, and that is why Aristotle, looking back over the history of Greek thought, could describe Plato as a Pythagorean. For if form is essentially something that differentiates itself into a hierarchy of forms, it is not necessary to suppose that mathematical forms, infinite though they are in their own diversity, exhaust the whole of this hierarchy: there may be non-mathematical forms as well.

§ 2. *Plato: The Theory of Forms*

(i) *Reality and intelligibility of the forms.* Form, differentiating itself into an infinite hierarchy of forms, was thus conceived by Pythagoreanism, and presumably by its founder, as constituting the nature of things. It was form in things that made them behave as they did behave, made them be what they were. Form or structure, not matter or that which is capable of taking on forms, was henceforth identified as essence. Relatively to the behaviour of the things in which it exists, form is essence or nature. Relatively to the human mind that studies it, form is not perceptible, like the things that go to make up the natural world: it is intelligible. As a plurality of forms it constitutes what may be called an intelligible world, *mundus intelligibilis*, νοητὸς τόπος.

This intelligible world is fully and in every sense real. Nothing could be farther from the thought of a Pythagoras or a Plato than the view that circularity or goodness is a mere idea in our minds, a creature of our human intellect, a νόημα or *ens rationis*. They are just as independent of the human thought which studies them as the earth and the stars and the other things that go to make up the world of nature.

If the word 'real' means the opposite of 'imaginary' or 'illusory', these 'ideas' (as they came to be called by Plato) were regarded as equally 'real' with bodily or material things. If 'real' is meant as a translation for the Greek ἀληθής, they are far more real. For ἀληθής in Greek means literally unhidden, unconcealed, undeceptive. To call a man ἀληθής means that he is candid, open, truthful about what he himself is, not a hypocrite. To call a thing ἀληθές means that it does not deceive people by making them think it is what it is not. We have the same sense of 'real' when we speak of 'real lace' or a 'real antique'.

Now, triangles and circles are things in which there is no deception. A mathematical circle is absolutely 'real' in the Greek sense; that is to say, it is really circular. Whereas a plate or cup is not, regarded as a circle, quite 'real'; because the potter cannot make it quite circular. It deceives the eye into thinking it a true circle when it is not.

The Platonic doctrine that perceptible things are unreal, or at least far less real than intelligible things or 'forms' or 'ideas', is difficult for modern readers to understand unless they will take the trouble to distinguish these two senses of the word 'real'. It would become easy to understand if people could see that it implies the same sense of the word 'real' which we use when we say 'This lace is real and that is not'.

It is for Plato a proof of the 'unreality' of the things which go to make up the natural world, that they are liable to change: not merely that they can be changed by the action upon them of external forces, but that they change of themselves, and thus show themselves to be inherently transitory: γιγνόμενα, he says,

not ὄντα. This shows them to be unreal, because it shows that
their hold upon their own ostensible characteristics is insecure.
The sun, for example, is a dying sun, and this is only a way of
saying that it has in it non-solar and indeed anti-solar characteristics, which are by degrees overcoming and ousting its solar
characteristics. It is not through and through genuinely a sun;
the prevalence in it, just now, of solar characteristics is only a
passing phase in an existence that is wholly made up of passing
phases. If Plato calls the sun unreal, he does not mean that
when we say 'There is the sun' there is in fact nothing there at
all; what he means is that the thing which is really there does
not possess, firmly and unconcealedly, the qualities which
when we call it the sun we think it to possess: these qualities it
only enjoys for the time being; they are not its inalienable
property; we think they are, but we are deceived.

Contrast this with the state of things in a mathematical
triangle or a mathematical circle. The triangle contains in
itself no hidden elements of untriangularity; the circle, no
hidden elements of non-circularity. If a perceptible body, like
a piece of iron, is hot, it is only hot to a certain extent. To say
that it is not hotter is a way of saying that there is still a certain
element of coldness in it. Even in the sun itself, the opposites
hot and cold coexist, and if one is hidden it is not on that account
absent. But the triangle or circle contains no hidden qualities
opposite to its own. It is purely or solely what it is. This is true
of all 'ideas' or 'forms' or 'intelligibles'; all of them are solely
what they are; whereas about all perceptible or bodily things
the truth is that they are a mixture of 'what they are'—their
ostensible characteristics, I have called these things—and
'what they are not', the opposites of their ostensible characteristics.

(ii) *Forms conceived first as immanent, later as transcendent.*
This is the way, or at any rate part of the way, in which we
find 'perceptibles' and 'intelligibles' related in the works of
Plato. There seem to be two stages in the Greek idea of that
relation. At first the intelligible form or 'idea' seems to have
been merely the formal element or structure of a thing which,
looked at as a whole, consisted of matter organized in a certain
way. The matter was that which underwent formation or
organization: the form was the way in which the matter was

organized. The world, the aggregate of natural things, was throughout its fabric a complex of matter and form. There was nowhere in the world any unformed matter, nowhere in the world any form not embodied in matter. Outside the world there might be. as the Ionians believed, unformed matter to an indefinite amount; but it did not follow that there was also disembodied form. Form was wholly immanent in the world. Form, the intelligible, had its being only as that which rendered intelligible the world in which it was immanent.

In addition to this view, however, we find in Greek philosophical literature another, according to which form is transcendent. Form is now conceived as having its being not in the perceptible world of nature at all, but 'by itself' (αὐτὸ καθ' αὑτό) in a separate world, not the perceptible world of material things but the intelligible world of pure forms.

This view of form as transcendent has been powerfully and elaborately stated by Plato in the *Symposium* and the *Phaedo*. Scholars who have analysed the language of the Platonic dialogues statistically, with a view to determining their relative date, have placed these two dialogues close together and have assigned them to the second of the four 'groups' into which they have divided the Platonic writings. Whatever view is taken of Platonic 'stylometry' in its more detailed development,[1] modern scholars are agreed that both the *Symposium* and the *Phaedo* were written in or soon after 385, when Plato had

---

[1] Lutoslawski, *The Origin and Growth of Plato's Logic* (London, 1897). His names for the four 'groups' (pp. 162–83) are (I) Socratic Group (*Apology, Euthyphro, Crito, Charmides, Laches, Protagoras, Meno, Euthydemus, Gorgias*); (II) First Platonic Group (*Cratylus, Symposium, Phaedo, Republic* i); (III) Middle Platonic Group (*Republic* ii–x, *Phaedrus, Theaetetus, Parmenides*); (IV) Latest Group (*Sophist, Politicus, Philebus, Timaeus, Critias, Laws*). Lutoslawski's work was a continuation and elaboration of researches set on foot by Lewis Campbell in 1867. It is now generally agreed that Campbell's methods were in principle sound, and that in its main lines the chronology of Plato's dialogues has been definitely established by their use. Thus A. E. Taylor (*Plato*, 1926, p. 19) accuses Lutoslawski of having 'pushed a sound principle to the pitch of absurdity in the attempt' to date every dialogue relatively to the rest, but admits and incorporates into his own work 'the broad discrimination between an earlier series of dialogues of which the *Republic* is the capital work and a later series'. And L. Robin (*Platon*, Paris, 1935, p. 37) in effect agrees both that the method of Campbell is sound and that Lutoslawski has been led by its attractions into a degree of detail which cannot be justified.

The date 385 is fixed by a reference in the *Symposium* to an event which happened in that year.

recently founded the Academy and was between 40 and 45 years old.

(iii) *Was the transcendence of the forms a Platonic conception?* It is possible that the conception of form as immanent was the original conception: the original Pythagorean conception, in the case of mathematical forms and the world of nature; the original Socratic conception, in the case of ethical forms and the world of human conduct. This seems likely on general grounds; for it would appear natural that, when people first think about form and its relation to matter, they should begin by thinking of it as correlative to matter and as existing only in things which have a material element as well. And it may have been Plato who first abandoned this original conception and first propounded the conception of form as transcendent.

Before looking at the evidence which might be used to support this suggestion, I will try to define the suggestion itself a little more precisely. Two qualifications must be borne in mind.

First, it must be understood that immanence and transcendence are not mutually exclusive conceptions. I have already pointed out, in connexion with the contrast between the transcendent magician-god of Thales and the immanent world-god of Anaximander (see p. 34, footnote 1), that a theology of pure transcendence is a thing as hard to find in the history of thought as a theology of pure immanence. All theologies have in fact both immanent and transcendent elements in them, though in this or that case this or that element may be obscured or suppressed. What is true in theology is equally true in the case of a metaphysical conception like form. The suggestion we are considering, therefore, is not that a purely immanent conception of form was replaced by a purely transcendent one, but that a conception in which immanence was emphasized gave way to one in which transcendence was emphasized: the relatively unemphasized element never being denied, or at least never being denied except by quite incompetent and muddle-headed persons.

Secondly, it must be understood that words like 'discovery', 'first', or 'novelty', when used in connexion with the history of philosophy, bear a rather special sense. Normally, a person who is said to 'make a philosophical discovery' in, say, his fortieth year would tell you, if you asked him, that he had known for a long time, perhaps all his life, the thing which he is said to have discovered; and that what he did in his fortieth year was not to discover it but to see for the first time, or to see more clearly and steadily than before, the connexions between it and certain other things; or else to see these connexions in a new light, as useful or clarifying connexions, having seen them hitherto as irksome and confusing connexions. Normally, again, a man who is said to have 'made a philosophical discovery' would tell you, if you asked him, that he had the idea from something that somebody else had written or said. Whether this forerunner fully understood what he was writing or saying is doubtful; but if he did, the discovery belongs to him, not to the man who gets the credit for it. And even if he did not, he deserves some share of the credit. Normally, I say, because how ready a man is to give someone else, or his own past self, the credit for having already known these things depends on his generosity, his candour, his readiness to admit his debt to other persons, or the debt of his present self to his past self, or the opposites of these qualities. Historically, there always are such debts, whether they are admitted or no. A man may be psychologically incapable of admitting them, and yet intellectually able to make important discoveries. But that is exceptional. Normally, important discoveries are made by people whose psychological condition with respect to these questions is a healthy one. If the man who took the momentous philosophical step of moving from a relatively immanent to a relatively transcendent conception of form was the same man who wrote the Platonic dialogues, he was a man of remarkable modesty and remarkable humour; the last man in the world to claim exclusive credit for his own discoveries; a man much likelier to over-estimate than to under-estimate the debt which in making them he owed to the predecessors whom he has so vividly and sympathetically brought before us on the stage of his theatre.

The suggestion we are considering, thus qualified, falls into two parts. First, that in early Pythagoreanism mathematical forms were conceived primarily though not exclusively as immanent, and that Plato worked out and consolidated, though he neither absolutely originated nor believed himself to have absolutely originated, a conception of them as primarily though not exclusively transcendent; and secondly, that in the humanistic philosophy of Socrates ethical forms were conceived as primarily though not exclusively immanent, and that Plato worked out and consolidated in the same way, and subject to the same qualifications, a conception of them as primarily transcendent.

(iv) *Participation and imitation.* With regard to the first point there is a curious piece of evidence in Aristotle's *Metaphysics*, 987ᵇ11-13: οἱ μὲν γὰρ Πυθαγόρειοι μιμήσει τὰ ὄντα φασὶν εἶναι τῶν ἀριθμῶν, Πλάτων δὲ μεθέξει, τοὔνομα μεταβαλών (the Pythagoreans say that things *imitate* numbers; Plato that they *participate* in them: a merely verbal change). This occurs in a passage dealing with Plato's philosophy and describing it as very much like Pythagoreanism in its general features but different from it in certain special ways. The general resemblance does not imply affiliation, for Aristotle himself says at the beginning of the same passage that Plato derived his philosophical views from early contact with the Heraclitean Cratylus and later association with Socrates (*Met.* 987ᵃ32 seqq.). The passage is curious because 'imitation' implies transcendence while 'participation' implies immanence. It is for this reason that Sir David Ross in his note on the sentence (*Aristotle's Metaphysics*, Oxford, 1924, vol. i, p. 162), calls it 'surprising that Aristotle should describe the change from μίμησις to μέθεξις as merely verbal' It would be less surprising if Plato's change of terminology had been intended to signalize the fact that the Pythagoreans had put forward an immanence-theory of form but had used a vocabulary which implied a transcendence-theory. In that case a post-Pythagorean who wished to put forward a transcendence-theory would find it necessary to distinguish more clearly than his predecessors between transcendence-language and immanence-language, and might very reasonably criticize the Pythagoreans for saying transcendence when they meant immanence.

There is independent evidence that Plato, when he began putting forward his own transcendence-theory, found a suitable terminology already in existence but used for a different purpose. In the *Phaedo* transcendence-phrases like αὐτὸ ὃ ἔστι and αὐτὸ καθ' αὑτό are freely used, as is well known, without explanation, as if they were already familiar; though whether this means familiar to a circle of Socratic hearers in 399 or to a circle of Platonic readers in 385 is another question. Obvious though this implied familiarity with transcendence-language is, however, it is still more obvious that no familiarity is implied with the transcendence-theory 'Socrates' expresses by using it. Either the audience, the 399 audience or the 385 audience, has been accustomed to hearing transcendence-language used for the expression of a very imperfectly thought-out transcendence-theory, or else they have heard it used for the expression of an immanence-theory. But these two alternatives are not really distinct. For it is something of an over-simplification to describe μίμησις or μέθεξις, αὐτὸ ὃ ἔστιν or αὐτὸ καθ' αὑτό, or indeed any other terms whatever, as 'transcendence-language' or 'immanence-language', as if their use implied transcendence or immanence only. Transcendence and immanence imply each other; and consequently μίμησις, which asserts transcendence, implies immanence, while μέθεξις, which asserts immanence, implies transcendence.

To say that a thing 'participates in' a form, or 'shares in' it, is to use a legal metaphor whose exact significance in such a context is not easy to estimate. The legal conception which is being metaphorically used is the conception of joint ownership; and the verb μετέχειν normally has a double object, an accusative of the share and a genitive of that which is shared. Thus, to say that a rose 'has its share of red' is to say that there is red in the rose, hence that red is immanent in the rose: but it is also to imply that there is other red which is not this rose's share and is therefore outside it. The other shares of red are, no doubt, in other roses. But what one is trying to describe in this legal metaphor is a state of things in which one and the same colour, red, is found in many different roses but remains one and the same wherever it is found; this is implied when one makes the statement that all these roses have their shares 'of red'. One is even implying that this single indivisible thing called 'red' is independent of there being any roses at all; just as the statement 'I have a share in the Great Western Railway', which asserts that the Great Western Railway is divisible and that I have a part of it, implies that the Great Western Railway is one and indivisible, a single business unit, and that this business unit is independent of there being any 'shareholders in' it, so that if all shareholders were abolished and it were confiscated by a socialist government it would still be the Great Western Railway.

If you say that a thing 'imitates' a form, you are saying that the form is not in the thing but outside it. But you are implying that the thing and the form which it imitates have something in common; for nothing can imitate any other thing except by having something in common with that other thing. What they 'have in common' is something in which they 'share'. For example, if you say that red is not shared out among roses but is a single and indivisible thing, an archetypal red independent of all the roses in the world, you will describe the relation between a given rose and this archetypal red by saying that the rose 'imitates' red. But when you ask how a rose could imitate red, you will have to answer: 'By having a colour of its own, namely a colour like enough to red to pass as an imitation of it'. And when you ask how like it must be, you must answer: 'As like as red is to red.' The rose can imitate red only because it has red in itself. As immanence implies transcendence, so transcendence implies immanence.

(v) *The Parmenides. Immanence and transcendence imply one another.* The mutual implication of transcendence and immanence is not only a truth, it is a truth which Plato discovered and expounded; though his exposition of it was only written down between fifteen and twenty years after he wrote his expositions of the transcendence-theory, and his discovery of it is there presented, characteristically enough, as a piece of tardy justice done to a great man who had taught it nearly a century ago.

The great man was Parmenides of Elea, and Plato acknowledges the debt which he owes to the Italian philosopher by publishing his discovery in a dialogue called after him and describing a conversation between him and Socrates which is feigned to have happened about 450 B.C. The dialogue was written soon after 369.[1]

The young Socrates begins (129) by stating and defending the immanence-theory of form, and describing the relation between

[1] On the dates see A. E. Taylor, *The Parmenides of Plato*, Oxford, 1934, pp. 1–4.

it and the things which are formed in the participation-language. Parmenides replies that this participation-language, if taken seriously, commits you to thinking of the form as divisible, in which case you have surrendered its unity; whereas if form is not one and indivisible it is nothing (131). The young Socrates, like so many philosophers in distress, takes refuge in a limited *ad hoc* subjective idealism: perhaps, he says, forms are only thoughts. Parmenides with one turn of a wrist pulls him out of that bolt-hole, and Socrates once more faces the music, this time by stating the transcendence-theory and using the imitation-language. Parmenides replies (with the rapidity and conclusiveness which are so characteristic of this dialogue, and give the lie to those who think Plato's growing absorption in philosophical problems is by now weakening his grip as a dramatic writer) that if anything is like the form it must have something in common with the form, and this 'something in common' is a second form, immanent of course; and if you convert this immanent form into a transcendent form you will need a third form, and so on; so the conversion of immanence (participation) into transcendence (imitation) does not solve our problem (132–3).

The arguments of Parmenides are conclusive as against both the immanence-theory and the transcendence-theory taken separately, as one-sided and mutually exclusive theories. They would have no weight against a theory in which immanence and transcendence were regarded as correlatives mutually implying each other. People who read them often fancy that no such third theory is possible; that any theory of form must be either a one-sidedly immanence-theory or a one-sidedly transcendence-theory; and that since Parmenides has exploded both these varieties of it, the 'Platonic Theory of Forms' is henceforth bankrupt. This is a mistake. What Parmenides has shown is not that the theory of forms is untenable, but that when you try to state such a theory in terms of immanence you are implying transcendence, and when you try to state it in terms of transcendence you are implying immanence.

It thus appears, I do not say proved, but probable from the evidence in our possession that the original Pythagorean conception of form in the world of nature was a conception framed chiefly, though not exclusively, in terms of immanence, the transcendence-element appearing, perhaps, mainly in the choice of vocabulary; and that Plato distinguished these two elements more clearly than his predecessors and began by emphasizing the element that had been neglected; perhaps by over-emphasizing it. Later it appears that Plato recognized the two elements to be logically interdependent.

With regard to the Socratic conception of form in the world of human activity the same thing seems to have happened. To quote Aristotle once more (*Met.* 1078^{b}30–1), 'Socrates did not make universals or definitions separable, but others separated them' ὁ μὲν Σωκράτης τὰ καθόλου οὐ χωριστὰ ἐποίει οὐδὲ τοὺς ὁρισμούς· οἱ δ' ἐχώρισαν. By 'others' Aristotle means Plato. This has been denied in the interests of a theory that the views propounded by 'Socrates' in the Platonic dialogues, or at any rate in a certain group of them which includes the *Symposium*, *Phaedo*, and *Republic*, were the views actually maintained by Socrates himself. According to that theory, the transcendence-conception expounded in those three dialogues must be Socratic in origin and the contrast asserted in this sentence between Socratic immanence and Platonic transcendence must be illusory. Sir David Ross, however, has shown conclusively (*Aristotle's Metaphysics*, cit., ii. 420–1), by comparing this passage in book *M* with what is practically a duplicate in book *A*, that 'others' does mean Plato, and that Aristotle is here telling us that ethical forms were regarded by Socrates as immanent, by Plato as transcendent.

(vi) *The influence of Cratylus.* If the conception of form in Pythagoreanism and in the philosophy of Socrates was in the first instance an immanence-conception, what was it that drove Plato towards the opposite extreme? Aristotle (*Met.* 987^{a}32) says that Plato in his youth was instructed in Heraclitean ideas by Cratylus. Elsewhere (*Met.* 1010^{a}7) he tells us that many people, starting from the Heraclitean doctrine of a universal flux, came to the sceptical conclusion that if everything was constantly changing no statement about anything could be true (περί γε τὸ πάντῃ πάντως μεταβάλλον οὐκ ἐνδέχεσθαι ἀληθεύειν). Consequently, says Aristotle, Cratylus ended by making up his mind never to speak at all: he only wagged his finger (οὐθὲν ᾤετο δεῖν λέγειν ἀλλὰ τὸν δάκτυλον ἐκίνει μόνον). From this scepticism, if he had ever in fact been influenced

by it, Plato would certainly have been rescued by Socrates.
A man who will decide, on philosophical grounds, to give up
speaking and confine himself to pointing must be a man in
whom the ordinary interests of intelligent human beings have
been completely strangled by the parasitic growth of a philosophy only capable of killing what it feeds on. Socrates was
a philosopher of the opposite kind; a philosopher whose
philosophy clarified and strengthened the interests out of
which it grew, especially the interest in λόγοι, the very things
Cratylus had renounced: λόγοι as conversations, λόγοι as statements, λόγοι as definitions, λόγοι as arguments, λόγοι as
reasons, λόγοι as proportions or ratios or forms. To a young
man who had come into contact with the varied and vigorous
intellectual life of Socrates, remembering Cratylus must have
been like remembering a ghost. Cratylus must have appeared
in retrospect as a man who had committed intellectual suicide
because he had got hold of the stick by the wrong end and had
not the strength of will to let go; Socrates, by contrast, was
obviously a man who lived and throve, with a huge appetite for
intellectual life, because his end of the stick was the right one.

The contrast plainly had something to do with the fact that
Cratylus was obsessed by the world of nature as we perceive it.
The perceptible world, as the Ionians knew, is a world of inces-
sant change. Heraclitus, true to the Ionian tradition, had said
that you cannot step twice into the same river. Cratylus—it is
the only saying of his that has been preserved—said Heraclitus
was wrong to think you could step into a river even once
(Aristotle, *Met*. 1010ᵃ15). Obsession by the perceptible, one
sees, had led him where it led William James. The world had
melted into a 'buzzing, blooming confusion'. What Plato
carried away from his training under Cratylus was quite clearly
the solid experimental knowledge that when you allow yourself
to be obsessed by the perceptible that is what happens to you.
I say 'quite clearly', because Plato's writings leave no doubt
about it. Over and over again Plato has given us vivid descriptions of the perceptible as a heaving, tossing, restless welter in
which a thing no sooner assumes a definite shape than it loses it
again. Thought finds here no rest for the sole of its foot. There is
nothing to know, because there is nothing definite. Socrates, however much he was aware of this heaving, tossing confusion of the

perceptible world, was not obsessed by it; because in the ethical inquiries in which Plato found him engaged he concerned himself not with the psychological processes involved in, for example, a man's attempt to be brave, but with the ideal of bravery which in that attempt the man set before himself. What, Socrates would ask, is this thing called bravery? What is its λόγος, its definition? By what λόγος, what process of thinking, reasoning, arguing, shall we try to discover that definition? Wagging your finger is here neither profitable nor necessary. It is not profitable, because it brings you no nearer understanding the nature of bravery; it is not necessary, because bravery is not a transitory phase of the psychological process, it is an ideal which the man keeps steadily before himself as that process develops.

Socrates, says Aristotle, 'did not separate' a form like that of bravery; he regarded such a form as 'ingredient' (I use Whitehead's terminology) 'in the occasions' in which it is manifested. This is the immanence-theory of form, the theory which in Plato's *Parmenides* the 'young Socrates' begins by putting forward. I suggest that Plato's movement from this immanence-theory to his own transcendence-theory was due to the need which he felt of protecting himself against the legacy of Cratylus. If the form of bravery is altogether immanent, if it is merely a passing form assumed for a moment and then relinquished again by the heaving, tossing confusion which we call the psychological processes involved in the attempt to be brave, the unity or indivisibility of that form is lost. In order that there should 'be something that we call bravery' (the phrase is a common one in Plato's writings) the thing we call bravery on one occasion must be the same as the thing we call bravery on another occasion; and the thing a man is setting before himself as an ideal while he is trying to be brave must be the same as the thing which he achieves at a later moment when he is being brave, or failing to achieve when he fails to be brave. In short: the Socratic analysis of ethical conceptions, which to Socrates himself revealed those conceptions as immanent in actions of certain kinds, to Plato revealed the same conceptions as transcendent: not merely as characteristics of certain classes of actions, but as ideals which the persons doing those actions held before themselves *as* ideals and to which the actions themselves were related not as instances but as approximations. In the extremest development of this transcendence-theory it was no longer maintained that there were or need be any instances at all: the Socratic ethical forms were conceived never as characters exemplified by this or that action but always and purely as ideals at which, in doing this or that action, the agent aimed. This provided a perfect protection against the scepticism which had overtaken Cratylus; and the more strongly Plato felt the influence of Cratylus working in his mind the more strongly he would emphasize, one supposes, the transcendence-element in his own conception of form. At the same time, it is easy to believe that the contrast between his own transcendence-theory and the immanence-theory of Socrates appeared to him much less acute than it did to Aristotle. The ideas which went to the making of his transcendence-theory were doubtless all present in the teaching of Socrates; only Socrates had not been through the mill of Cratylus' scepticism, and therefore was not obliged to pick them out and weld them together and organize them into a deliberately framed and deliberately held theory of transcendence. That is why Plato, in the *Symposium* and *Phaedo*, was able to put into the mouth of Socrates the very doctrine which, according to Aristotle, constituted his own chief divergence from Socrates' teaching.

Later, when the early impress of Cratylus had been by these means overcome in Plato's mind, he could see that the transcendence-theory of the *Symposium* and *Phaedo* had been an exaggeration. There was no longer any need to select for special emphasis the transcendence-elements in the thought of Socrates, because that selection and that emphasis had done their work. This was the frame of mind in which he wrote the *Parmenides*.

(vii) *The influence of Parmenides*. Whether Parmenides himself, and the Eleatic school which he founded, had any positive influence on Plato's early development it is not easy to say. Aristotle does not help us. Plato himself does not help us very much. But it is more than possible that the transcendence-theory of Plato's early middle age was conditioned by Eleatic teaching. Parmenides, in the considerable fragments which have come down to us, makes a distinction between two ways of thinking, the Way of Truth and the Way of Belief. Belief is regarded as containing no truth: to believe is to be deceived, and a Way of Belief means a way of thinking in which the thinker is systematically and incessantly deluded.

With this introduction Parmenides has already asserted a kind of transcendence-theory. Truth is not, he has told his readers, immanent in Belief, as a kind of leaven leavening the lump of error. Belief is mere belief and consequently sheer error. Truth is quite different from it, and is under no obligation to come to terms with it. Truth has to be reached by sheer thinking, and sheer thinking pays no attention to the plausibilities of Belief. Here Parmenides is expounding what may be called a transcendence-conception of methodology or epistemology, according to which thought, as the successful pursuit of truth, is related by way of transcendence to the unsuccessful pursuit of truth which is called Belief.

This leads up to a transcendence-conception of the world. That which *is*, Parmenides argues, cannot have come into existence in the past, and it cannot be going to perish in the future. It must be one; that is to say, in addition to what *is* there cannot be anything else. Here 'the one that *is*' means the physical or material world; what Parmenides is saying is that this world cannot have a beginning or an end, it must be eternal, and it cannot have either within it or outside it any empty space. The world is a continuous homogeneous indivisible *plenum*, of which and within which there can be no motion. This is the real world, the true world, the world as we know it to be when we think clearly, in other words the intelligible world. The world of differentiated substances, the world of change and motion, the world of coming-into-existence and of passing-away, in short the perceptible world, is the world of Belief. It is not, as the Ionians thought, reality; it is the delusion which we impose upon ourselves by thinking amiss.

It is impossible not to find echoes of this in the Platonic dialogues of the transcendence-group, especially the *Republic*. We find there the same distinction between two ways of thinking, called Knowledge (ἐπιστήμη) and Belief (δόξα); the same insistence that what most people take for knowing is only believing; the same conviction that believing is being deceived by the unstable and indeterminate world of perceptibles, and the same conviction that the only reality, the only thing that does not deceive us, is the imperceptible or intelligible object of knowledge.

(viii) *Plato's mature conception of the forms.* Where Plato differs sharply from the Eleatics is that for them the real or intelligible is a physical world but a 'paradoxical' one, that is, one having characteristics opposite to those which we find in the physical world we perceive; whereas for Plato the real or intelligible is not physical at all, it is pure form without any matter; physicality is for Plato one characteristic of the perceptible, and whatever is physical is to that extent not intelligible.

With this difference goes another. By identifying the intelligible with form, Plato has abolished the Parmenidean distinction between the physical world as it appears to us in perception and the physical world as revealed to us by thought. He has abolished, in other words, the distinction between the physical world, or world of nature, as we falsely conceive it according to the evidence of our senses and that same world as we truly know it by sheer thinking. Plato's doctrine is that all there is to know about the physical or natural world is known to us by perception; perception is therefore not a way of deluding ourselves about things which could be more effectively studied in a different way; it is the best way there is of studying things which because they are always changing have no determinate characters and therefore cannot strictly speaking be known, or understood, at all; but that is no reason why we should not observe them with care and even understand whatever in them is intelligible, namely the formal elements which are immanent in them. Thus even in his most one-sidedly transcendent phase Plato by anticipation defends, as against the Eleatics, what we nowadays call the empirical sciences of nature, that is, the collection and organization of perceptually observed natural facts; and when he has passed beyond this one-sidedly transcendent phase he even defends by anticipation a science of nature that is more than merely empirical: a science of nature which not merely observes and classifies brute facts, but finds in the natural world itself structural or formal elements which, so far as they are formal, are intelligible in their own right.

This implies a theory of the relation between form and the world of nature which is neither merely a transcendence-theory nor merely an immanence-theory. Some combination of transcendence and immanence, I have insisted, was present from the start in both the Pythagorean and the Socratic conceptions of form; but Plato seems to have been the first person to distinguish clearly between the transcendence-conception of form and the immanence-conception, and until the two were clearly distinguished the question how they could be combined did not arise. The way in which Plato seems to have combined them is this. Form, whether mathematical or ethical, when understood in all its rigour, is transcendent and not immanent. When we say that a plate is round or an action just, we never mean that the plate is absolutely round or the action absolutely just. Absolute roundness is a pure transcendent form apprehended by the potter who makes the plate, and apprehended too by a man who looks at the plate: by the potter, because he is trying to make the plate as round as he can, and therefore must know what roundness as such, absolute roundness, is; by the man who looks at the plate, because the plate (in Platonic terms) 'reminds' him of roundness as such or absolute roundness. In both cases there is a connexion between the plate and true or absolute roundness. But this connexion is not immanence. The plate's shape is not an instance of true or absolute roundness. In spite of all that has been said to the contrary, the Platonic form is not a 'logical universal', and the things, in the natural world or the world of human conduct, to which it stands in a one-many relation are not instances, or what we sometimes called 'particulars', of it. The shape of the plate is an instance not of roundness but of approximation to roundness.

Thus the form that is immanent in perceptibles, the form which is a 'logical universal', of which these perceptibles are instances or 'particulars', is not pure form, as pure form is understood by mathematical or ethical thought; it is only an approximation to that pure form. The structure or form which is 'in' natural things or in human actions, constitutes their essence, and is the source of their general or special characteristics, is not the pure form itself, it is a tendency to approximate to this pure form. What plates and wheels and planetary orbits have in common, what is immanent in them all as that in which they participate, is not circularity, but a tendency towards circularity. What different legal decisions have in common is not justice itself but an attempt on the part of the courts that make these decisions to arrive at a just decision. Such attempts are never wholly successful, and that is why the pure form remains transcendent. If they were wholly successful, it would be immanent as well as transcendent. Because they are never wholly successful, the transcendent form remains purely transcendent, and the immanent form remains a mere 'imitation' or approximation.

Neoplatonists at a much later date asked why these attempts to embody the pure form are never wholly successful, and said that it was owing to the recalcitrance of matter, which would not take form upon itself with perfect plasticity. Thus matter was identified by the Neoplatonists with the cause of imperfection, defective organization, or, in general, evil. This idea is neither expressed nor implied in the writings of Plato himself. For him, the question why such attempts always partially fail does not arise. It is a simple matter of fact that they do always partially fail.

§ 3. *Plato's cosmology: the Timaeus*

The cosmology which was developed under the influence of these conceptions has been stated for us by Plato in the *Timaeus*. It has generally been assumed that Plato was there putting forward his own cosmological views; but Professor Taylor, in great detail and with great learning, has argued[1] that he was not doing this but was expounding the Pythagorean doctrine of the late fifth century. For our present purpose it does not matter which hypothesis we adopt; and the more seriously we take Aristotle's description of Plato as a Pythagorean the less it matters for any purpose; so with this warning I shall give a sketch of the cosmological doctrine contained in the *Timaeus*.

The main lines of Ionian thought are reproduced to this extent, that the material or perceptible world is still conceived as a living organism or animal made by God. But conformably to the Pythagorean revolution the emphasis has shifted from the idea of matter to the idea of form. Timaeus never explicitly

[1] *A Commentary on Plato's Timaeus* (Oxford, 1928).

says that God made the world out of, or in, a pre-existing matter; and so little stress is laid on matter throughout the dialogue that Professor Taylor has boldly pronounced the cosmology of the *Timaeus* to be a cosmology without matter, a cosmology where everything material is resolved into pure form. This is perhaps going too far; at any rate, it goes so far as to conflict with his own view that the *Timaeus* is Pythagorean; for other sources show that the Pythagorean cosmology did undoubtedly use the idea of matter, though not the idea of a matter which could be rarefied and condensed. The matter of the *Timaeus* is simply that which is capable of assuming geometrical form; and the form which it can receive is independent of any such material embodiment and constitutes in itself and apart from matter an intelligible world. This intelligible world is a presupposition of God's creative act, and is the eternal and changeless model upon which God made the temporal and changing world of nature. The world of nature is a material organism or animal, alive everywhere with spontaneous movement; the intelligible world is called an immaterial organism or animal: alive, because the forms are dynamically related to each other in virtue of the dialectical connexions between them, but not alive with movement, because movement implies space and time, and the world of forms has in it no space or time.

The problem at once arises, if there is neither space nor time in the world of forms, whence do they originate as features of the world of nature? For that world is called a copy or imitation of the world of forms; and one would expect any feature in it therefore to correspond with a feature in the model. To answer this, we must take space and time separately.

Space, in the *Timaeus*, corresponds to no feature of the intelligible world. Space is simply that out of which the copy is made; it is like the sculptor's clay or the draughtsman's paper. The argument of the *Timaeus* contains no attempt at a deduction of space. Just as the Ionians started their cosmogony from the assertion of matter as a given fact, or rather the assertion of matter and space as two given facts, in so far as they held matter to be capable of condensation and rarefaction, so the *Timaeus* begins its cosmogony with space, or (as we might equally well say) with matter, for matter and space are not at this stage differentiated. The *Timaeus* does not eliminate matter, as Professor Taylor thinks: it identifies it with space as the receptacle of forms, and presupposes it. When I say that space is presupposed and not deduced, what I mean can be stated in the language of the *Timaeus* by saying that no attempt is made in the dialogue to show that God *made* space.

With time it is otherwise. Time, according to the explicit doctrine of the dialogue, is not a presupposition of God's creative act. It is one of the things He created. Consequently it must be created on some model; that is, it must correspond to some feature of the intelligible world. It came into existence, says Timaeus, simultaneously with the world of nature, so that there was no abyss of eventless time before creation, and creation was itself not an event in time: it is an eternal act, not a temporal event. According to a well-known but difficult expression, time was created as the moving image of eternity. What does this mean? First, time is a feature of the natural and material world, and everything in that world is involved in the general process of change. Time therefore is involved in that process: it passes or lapses. Secondly, everything in that world is a copy of something in the intelligible world; so time must be a copy of some feature in the intelligible world which corresponds to the lapse of time in the sensible world. But what is it that does so correspond? Not timelessness, for that is a mere negation, and, so far, nothing; it must be something positive. This positive something is eternity, regarded not as the mere absence of time (still less, of course, as an infinite amount of time) but as a mode of being which involves no change or lapse, because it contains everything necessary to itself at every moment of its own existence.

In the perceptible world the total nature of a thing is never realized all at once. An animal, for example, is something to which sleeping and waking are equally natural; but an animal cannot be asleep and awake at once; it can only realize these two parts of its nature at different times, by shifting over from one to the other. In the intelligible world everything realizes its entire nature simultaneously: all the properties of a triangle, for example, are present in the triangle at any given moment. The eternity of the triangle is the fact of its possessing all its properties at once, so that it does not need a lapse of time to realize them one after another. Temporal succession is the

'moving image' of this timeless self-enjoyment which charac-
terizes every part of the intelligible world.

If the world of nature is as old as time itself, and therefore
never came into existence at any given moment, why (we may
ask) should it not be regarded as existing of itself and in its own
right? Why must we look outside it for a creator; and why
should we not discard God from our cosmology? Timaeus'
answer is that the entire world of nature is a becoming or process,
and that all becoming must have a cause (τῷ γενομένῳ φαμὲν
ὑπ' αἰτίου τινὸς ἀνάγκην εἶναι γενέσθαι, 28 c). To this argument Kant
would reply that it is sophistical (or as he calls it, dialectical),
because it involves misusing a category whose proper function
is to relate one phenomenon to another phenomenon, by using
it to relate the sum total of phenomena to something that is not
a phenomenon: in other words, the relation between effect and
cause is a relation between one becoming or process and another;
it cannot be used to relate the totality of processes to something
not a process. From Kant's point of view, the statement of
Timaeus that all becoming must have a cause is ambiguous.
If *all becoming* means *any given case of becoming*, the statement
is true, and the cause will be another case of becoming, antecedent to it. If *all becoming* means *the totality of becomings*, as of
course it does for Timaeus, Kant will say that the statement
is not so much false as entirely baseless and in the last resort
meaningless.

But this criticism does not remove the difficulty. It only holds
good if the word 'cause' has its eighteenth-century meaning,
first definitely established in metaphysics by Hume, of an event
antecedent to and necessarily connected with another event
called the effect. To a Greek, anything goes by the name
'cause' which in any of the various senses of that word provides
an answer to a question beginning with the word *why*. As we
all know, Aristotle was to distinguish four senses of that word,
and hence four kinds or orders of cause: material, formal,
efficient, and final. And not one of these was regarded as an
event prior in time to its effect. Even the efficient cause, for
Aristotle, is not an event, but a substance which is the seat of
power: thus the efficient cause of a new organism is not the
event or act of generation but the parent which did that act.
If then we ask why there is a world of nature, we are asking a

question which does not necessarily involve the fallacy of applying the category of causation, understood as Kant and Hume understood it, to something outside the realm of phenomena and possible experience. Indeed we are asking a question which Kant himself thought it legitimate to ask and to which he gave a very original and important answer by saying that the understanding makes nature: a question which we must ask as soon as we realize that the world of nature does not explain itself, but presents itself to us as a complex of facts demanding explanation. There is certainly one way of explaining these facts by exhibiting the relations between them: that is, explaining any one of them in terms of the rest; but there is another kind of explanation which is equally necessary, namely explaining why facts of the kind we call natural should exist at all: this is what Kant called metaphysics of nature, and this is the type of inquiry to which the *Timaeus* belongs.

If then we are to ask why there is a world of change, a perceptible or natural world, at all, is it necessary to find the source of this world in a creative God? Cannot the unchanging source of change be identified with the forms? Clearly, Timaeus thinks this impossible: there must for him be a God as well as the intelligible world of forms, but why? He has not told us; but, later, the answer was given by Aristotle. It is that the forms are not ἀρχαὶ κινήσεως, not sources of change or efficient causes, but only formal and final causes: they do not originate change, they only regulate changes initiated elsewhere. They are standards, not agencies. Hence we must look elsewhere for the active source of movement and life in the world; and this can only be an agent whose acts are not events, an eternal agent which is not part of the natural world, something for which the proper name is God.

Timaeus next asks why God should have created any world at all. The reason he gives is that God is good, and the nature of goodness is to overflow outside itself and reproduce itself. As he puts it, goodness excludes envy; and this implies that what is good not only values itself for its own goodness but will not be content to enjoy that goodness exclusively, but must by its own nature bestow it on something else. This argument implies that there is something else on which to bestow it; in other words, that logically (though of course not temporally) prior to God's creation of the world there was, or rather is, a world or chaos of unformed matter which is the possible recipient of form and therefore of goodness. Professor Taylor, holding as he does that the concept of matter plays no part in the cosmology of the *Timaeus*, is obliged to explain this argument away, contending that the language is intentionally mythological and that no Pythagorean would have taken it as literal. But what is the doctrine which the mythological language is intended to convey? He has not told us, and for myself I can see no reason why Timaeus should, for this one paragraph, have spoken in parables without any warning. It is more likely that he meant what he said. God in the *Timaeus* is, after all, a δημιουργός, a maker or craftsman; his creative act is in any case not an act of absolute creation, for it presupposes something other than itself, namely the model upon which he makes the world; and if the absolute or perfectly free creativity of God is already surrendered by the doctrine that He made the world upon a pre-existing model, there is no further loss and no further inconsistency in maintaining that He made it out of a pre-existing matter. Indeed, if the model or form pre-existed to the act of copying it, the matter must have pre-existed too; for matter and form are correlative terms, and if the making of something is conceived as presupposing the form of that thing it must logically presuppose also its matter. The act of making the thing is then conceived quite logically as the imposition of this form upon this matter.

Professor Taylor, in denying that the concept of matter is implied by the cosmology of the *Timaeus*, is in fact twisting Plato, as throughout his work he is visibly anxious to do, into conformity with certain modern views which he admires and shares. It is almost impossible to expound ancient philosophers without falling into this kind of error; and no doubt we all do it. In this case, the error is to forget that the idea of absolute creation, of a creative act which presupposes nothing at all, whether a pre-existing matter or a pre-existing form, is an idea which originated with Christianity and constitutes the main characteristic differentiation distinguishing the Christian idea of creation from the Hellenic (and, for that matter, from the Hebrew idea of it expounded in the book of Genesis).

Timaeus next shows how different elements arise necessarily

within an extended and visible world. Extended means three-dimensional; therefore all measurements in the material world must be measurements of volume or cubic. Visibility implies fire or light, matter in the form of radiation; but the material world must also be tangible, and this implies matter in the form of solids. These qualitatively distinct forms of matter, true to the Pythagorean tradition, are based on mathematically distinct types of structure. Let the unit of radiation be called a^3, and the unit of solid matter b^3; then between these two extremes there are two mean proportionals, a^2b and ab^2, which give the two intermediate forms of matter, the gaseous and the fluid. The world is thus made of the four Empedoclean elements, deduced from a mathematical principle in a typically Pythagorean manner (and therefore, because deduced, not really elements as Empedocles conceived them); and the whole which they compose, it is argued, must be spherical, because the sphere is the only uniform solid and therefore any deviation from sphericity must be caused by some external influence—pressure, attraction, or the like—which *ex hypothesi* cannot be present.

So much for the body of the world. Timaeus next considers the creation of its soul, which he describes as transfusing the whole body and overlapping it externally like an envelope, so that the body of the world is as it were swathed in its own soul. For the soul belongs to a peculiar order of being: it is inter-mediate between the material world, or nature as a complex of processes, and the immaterial world, or nature as a permanent and indivisible complex of forms; hence it is both in the world and also outside it, as a man's soul both pervades his body and also reaches beyond it in the range of his sight, hearing, and thought. This passage is full of difficulties, and I shall not here stop to analyse it; I will only point out that in it Plato or Timaeus is trying to do two things: first, to show how the system of planetary movements and distances may be deduced, like the table of the four elements, from mathematical con-siderations, and secondly to show how the life which expresses itself in such a system of movements can also be a sentient and thinking life generating in itself thoughts and judgements.

At this point I must break off my analysis, offering what I have given as a sample of the Pythagorean method in cosmo-logy. In leaving the *Timaeus* I should like to mention the high opinion held of it, as a body of cosmological doctrine, by Whitehead, whose judgement deserves the utmost respect as that of one of the greatest living philosophers and perhaps the greatest living writer on cosmology. In Whitehead's opinion the *Timaeus* comes nearer than any other book to providing the philosophical setting required by the ideas of modern physical science. Certainly it comes very near to coinciding with the general cosmological views of Whitehead himself. In both cases the world of nature is a complex of movements, or processes in space and time, presupposing another complex, namely a world of forms, which Whitehead calls eternal objects, not in space or time. There are of course differences between the two views, some of them very important: I shall have more to say of them later, but I will shortly mention two or three points of divergence now.

(1) For Plato, or Timaeus, the things of the visible world are modelled upon the forms; but this is as close as they get. No planetary movement, for example, actually reproduces the mathematical curve to which it is an approximation. For Whitehead, the eternal objects are actually, as he calls it, ingredient in the transient phenomena. The visible world is no mere approximation to the intelligible: it just *is* the intelligible world realized here and now.

(2) Consequently, for Whitehead, any quality found in the world of nature must be an eternal object having its place in the eternal world of forms: the blueness of this patch of sky or the smell of this onion is just as much an eternal object as equality or justice. Whereas, for the *Timaeus*, many qualities found in the visible world might be, so to speak, by-products of the fact that this world is *not* an exact copy of the intelligible world.

(3) For the *Timaeus*, the soul of the world pervades its entire body, and thus the world as a whole is conceived as apprehending by its thought the eternal forms upon which its movements are modelled. For Whitehead, minds are one special class of phenomena, percipient occasions he calls them, so that mind for him instead of pervading the world of nature appears here and there at special places and times within it. This is a difference of doctrine which is characteristic of the whole difference between the Greek and the modern conceptions of nature.

III

ARISTOTLE

I NEXT pass to the cosmology of Aristotle, as expounded in Book *Λ* of the *Metaphysics*. Professor Jaeger, in his great book on the development of Aristotle's thought, argued that this book was an early work written under Platonic influence and in effect superseded as Aristotle's thought became less theological and more scientific and positive. This view has been effectively criticized by Mr. W. K. C. Guthrie of Cambridge, who in two articles in the *Classical Quarterly* (1933–4) has shown that Book *Λ* bears the marks of late composition and mature development, and has argued that Aristotle actually worked his way to the conclusions there advanced through a phase in which his thought was purely materialistic.

§ 1. *Meaning of φύσις*

Before considering the doctrine of Book *Λ* it is necessary to analyse the passage in Book *Δ* where Aristotle discusses the meaning of the word *φύσις*. Aristotle has a characteristic method in philosophical lexicography. He recognizes that a single word has several different meanings, and never falls into the stupid mistake of supposing that one word means one thing: on the other hand, he recognizes that these various meanings are connected among themselves, and that the word is not equivocal because it has more than one meaning. He thinks that of its various meanings one is the deepest and truest meaning; the others are approximations to it arising from varying degrees of failure to grasp this deepest meaning. Consequently he arranges his meanings in a series like shots on a target which gradually creep in and find the bull.

He distinguishes seven meanings of the word *φύσις*.

(1) *Origin or birth*: 'as if', says he, 'the *υ* were pronounced long.' The *υ* is actually short; and Sir David Ross (op. cit., ad loc.) points out that in actual Greek literature the word never has this meaning and conjectures, no doubt rightly, that this is a sense speculatively forced upon the word by mistaken

etymologizing in the fourth century. Thus the first shot recorded by Aristotle misses the target altogether.

(2) That out of which things grow, their *seed*. This again is a meaning nowhere found in Greek: I imagine it is put in as a link between the first meaning and the third.

(3) The *source of movement or change* in natural objects (we shall see later that a natural object is one which moves itself). This is the meaning when we say that a stone falls, or that fire rises, by nature: it corresponds to the ordinary untechnical Greek usage.

(4) The *primitive matter* out of which things are made. This is the sense emphasized by the Ionians. Burnet would regard it as the only sense which the word had in early Greek philosophy.

It would be truer, I think, to say that in sixth-century philosophy φύσις meant what it always did mean, namely the essence or nature of things; but that the Ionians, by a philosophical peculiarity, not a lexicographical one, tried to explain the essence or nature of things in terms of the stuff out of which they were made. (Cf. above, pp. 45 ff.)

(5) *The essence or form of natural things.* This is how we find the word actually used both in philosophy and in ordinary Greek, in fifth-century writers; but the definition is faulty because circular. To define nature as the essence of natural things leaves the term 'natural things' undefined.

(6) *Essence or form* in general. Plato, e.g., speaks of ἡ τοῦ ἀγαθοῦ φύσις, and the good is not a natural thing. The circle is here removed, but in Aristotle's opinion the term is now being too widely and loosely used: so he proceeds to narrow it again, but removes the circle by defining the term 'natural things' as meaning 'things that have a source of movement in themselves'.

(7) *The essence of things which have a source of movement in themselves.* This Aristotle regards as the true and fundamental meaning, and this, therefore, is how he uses the word himself. It certainly does accurately correspond with the ordinary Greek usage. When a Greek writer contrasts φύσις with τέχνη (i.e. what things are when left to themselves with what human skill can make of them) or φύσις with βία (how things behave when left to themselves with how they behave when interfered with) he implies that things have a principle of growth, organization, and movement, in their own right and that this is what he

means by their nature; and when he calls things natural he means that they have such a principle in them.

§ 2. *Nature as self-moving*

The world of nature is thus for Aristotle a world of self-moving things, as it is for the Ionians and for Plato. It is a living world: a world characterized not by inertia, like the world of seventeenth-century matter, but by spontaneous movement. Nature as such is process, growth, change. This process is a development, i.e. the changing takes successive forms $\alpha, \beta, \gamma, \ldots$ in which each is the potentiality of its successor; but it is not what we call 'evolution', because for Aristotle the kinds of change and of structure exhibited in the world of nature form an eternal repertory, and the items in the repertory are related logically, not temporally, among themselves. It follows that the change is in the last resort cyclical; circular movement is for him characteristic of the perfectly organic, not as for us of the inorganic.

Since nature is self-moving, it is illogical to postulate an efficient cause outside nature to account for the changes that take place in it. No doubt if there had been a time when nature did not yet exist, an efficient cause outside it would have been necessary to bring it into existence; but Aristotle follows the *Timaeus* in holding that there never was such a time. The process of the world is for him therefore exactly what Plato in the *Timaeus* said it could not be, namely a self-causing and self-existing process.

This looks as if Aristotle had thrown in his lot with the materialists, of whom Aristophanes wrote that Zeus is dethroned and Vortex reigns in his stead. But in *Met. Λ* God is reintroduced into cosmology by an entirely new argument. In order to be a materialist on these lines, one would have to hold, as many modern thinkers have held and some still do hold, that the laws of nature are merely empirical descriptions of the ways in which things actually do happen. There are bodies in motion; they must move somehow; and the ways in which as it happens they do move are called by us laws of nature, where by calling them laws we do not imply a lawgiver or ascribe to them any imperative or compulsive force, but merely signify their *general* character. But Greek thought never adopted this position.

Nature, for the Greeks, was characterized not merely by change but by effort or nisus or tendency, a tendency to change in certain definite ways. The seed is pushing its way up through the soil, the stone pressing down upon it; the young animal is working at increasing its size and developing its shape until it reaches the size and shape of an adult, and then its effort, having reached the goal, ceases. All process involves a distinction between the potential and the actual, and the potential is the seat of a nisus in virtue of which it is forcing its way towards actuality. This conception of nisus as a factor running through the entire natural world, with its teleological implications about ends towards which natural processes are directed, was at one time rejected by modern science as a piece of anthropomorphism. But it is by no mean an anthropomorphic idea, unless we falsely identify nisus with conscious volition. No doubt it would be anthropomorphic in the worst sense to credit the seed with a knowledge of what it is trying to do, an imagination of itself as a full-grown plant; but because the seed does not know that it is trying to become a plant we are not entitled to say that it is not unconsciously trying to do so. There is no ground for thinking unconscious effort an impossibility. And more recently the theory of evolution has necessitated a return to something not altogether unlike the Aristotelian theory of potentiality. It is widely recognized that a process of becoming is conceivable only if that which is yet unrealized is affecting the process as a goal towards which it is directed, and that mutations in species arise not through the gradual working of the laws of chance but by steps which are somehow directed towards a higher form— that is, a more efficient and vividly alive form—of life. In this respect, if modern physics is coming closer to Plato as the great mathematician-philosopher of antiquity, modern biology is coming closer to its great biologist-philosopher Aristotle, and evolutionary philosophies like those of Lloyd Morgan, Alexander, and Whitehead are frank in their acceptance of the ideas of potentiality, nisus, and teleology.

The conception of development is fatal to materialism. According to a materialistic metaphysics, that is to say, a metaphysics according to which bodily existence is the only kind of existence, whatever works or produces results must be a body: in other words, there can be no immaterial causes.

But development implies an immaterial cause. If a seed is really developing into a plant, and not merely changing into it by pure chance owing to the random impact of suitable particles of matter from outside, this development is controlled by something not material, namely the form of a plant, and of that specific plant, which is the Platonic idea of the plant as the formal cause of the full-grown plant and the final cause of the process by which the seed grows into it. This idea, of course, is not an idea in the ordinary English sense of a thought in somebody's mind. It does not exist in the mind of the plant; for if the plant has a mind at all, it has not the sort of mind that is capable of conceiving abstract ideas. It is an idea in the technical Platonic sense, something objectively real but not material.

So far, we are following Plato; but Aristotle now takes a step beyond him. For Plato, the energy which is canalized by the idea is not excited by it but exists independently of it. The origin of this energy is due to an efficient cause; and Plato's doctrine, if expressed in Aristotelian language, is that though the formal and final causes may be identical the efficient cause is something quite different from them. The mere crude force which works in the growth of a seed is one thing and the controlling influence which directs that force into the production of a plant is another. Aristotle, on the contrary, conceives the notion of a final cause which not only directs but also excites or awakens the energy which it controls, by arousing in the appropriate object a nisus towards its own realization in bodily form. It is thus both a final cause and an efficient: but an efficient cause of a very peculiar kind, an immaterial efficient cause. And Aristotle arrives at this conception of an immaterial efficient cause by reflection on the fact of development: for development implies nisus, that is, a movement or process not merely orientated towards the realization in bodily form of something not yet so realized, but actually motived by the tendency towards such realization. The seed only grows *at all* because it is working at becoming a plant; hence the form of a plant is the cause not only of its growing in that way but of its growing at all, and is therefore the efficient as well as the final cause of its growth. The seed grows only because it *wants* to become a plant. It desires to embody in itself, in material shape, the form of a plant which otherwise has a merely ideal or immaterial existence. We can use these words 'want' or 'desire' because although the plant has no intellect or mind and cannot conceive the form in question it has a soul or ψυχή and therefore has wants or desires, although it does not *know* what it wants. The form is the object of these desires: in Aristotle's own words, it is not itself in motion (for it is not a material thing and therefore of course cannot be in motion) but it causes motion in other things by being an object of desire: κινεῖ ὡς ἐρώμενον (1072ᵇ3).

Now the desire of the material thing is a desire to embody this form in its own matter, to conform itself to it and to imitate it, as well as possible, in that matter. The form, in order to excite such desire, must already be in its own right something worth imitating, something having an activity of its own which is inherently valuable. What kind of activity can we ascribe to the immaterial being which is in this sense the unmoved first mover of the natural world?

§ 3. Aristotle's theory of knowledge

In order to answer this question we must turn to Aristotle's theory of knowledge. Long before his time the Greeks had discovered that sound is a rhythmical vibration set up by a sonorous body and transmitted by the air to the mechanism of hearing. The essence of this mechanism is that it is a part of the organism which picks up the vibrations from the air and vibrates itself in the same rhythm. Any sound having a rhythm which our ears cannot reproduce in themselves is inaudible to us. To reproduce in myself a rhythmical vibration of this kind, and to hear a sound, are the same thing; because, for the Greeks, the soul is nothing but the vital activities of the body, and therefore the gulf which exists in modern thought between the bodily vibrations of the aural mechanism and the mental sensation of sound was for them non-existent. Now, the bronze of the bell, and the gases of the air, do not enter into my organism; but the rhythm of their vibrations does enter into it; and it is precisely this entrance of the rhythm into my head which is my hearing of the sound. But a rhythm is a Pythagorean or Platonic form; it is an immaterial thing, a type of structure, or in Aristotle's language a λόγος. To hear a ringing bell, then, is to receive into one's own organism the λόγος of the ringing bell without its ὕλη; and this, generalized, gives us Aristotle's definition of sensation. The ringing of the bell, its rhythmical vibration, reproduces itself in my head; and that is hearing. Similarly with sight and the other senses. In every case there is a perceived object, which is a certain kind of matter possessing whether permanently or temporarily a certain form: to perceive that object is to reproduce the form in ourselves while the matter remains outside ourselves. Hence Aristotle's definition of sense as the reception of sensible form without its matter.

This is not a representational or copy-theory of perception. It would be false to say that on Aristotle's view what we hear is the ringing in our head, which resembles the ringing of the bell in pitch and tone. For the note of the bell is nothing but a λόγος or rhythm: it simply *is* the rhythm of 480 vibrations a second or whatever it may be. Consequently the note ringing in our head is not another note like that of the bell, it is the very same note; precisely as the equation $(x+y)^2 = x^2+2xy+y^2$ is the very same equation when $x = 2$ and $y = 3$ that it is when $x = 3$ and $y = 4$. The note is not matter, it is form; true, a form which, to exist, must exist in some matter; but it is the same form in whatever matter it exists.

Now sensation is a kind of cognition; not a perfect kind, because in hearing the bell we only hear its note, and do not hear its shape or colour or chemical composition. But to this extent it is a fair example of cognition, that what we do hear is a form and that the way in which we hear it is by receiving that form into our organ of hearing. Suppose now there were a kind of knowledge whose object was a form not embodied in any matter: for example, the form of the good, assuming that there is such a thing. If we apprehend that form by thought, we can only do so by receiving it into our mind, experiencing it as a way in which our mind is organized for the time being, just as we hear a note by experiencing it as a way in which our ear is organized for the time being. In the case of the bell, the bronze remains outside us; but in the case of the good, where there is no matter, only form, nothing remains outside us; the entire object reproduces itself (not a copy of itself, but its very self) in our intellect. Hence, as Aristotle puts it, in the case of objects where there is no matter, the knower and the known are identical.

§ 4. *Aristotle's theology*

In the light of this idea let us look back at the distinction drawn in the *Timaeus* between God as eternal thinker, subject, mind, and the forms as eternal immaterial objects. God in the *Timaeus* certainly thinks the forms; therefore, according to Aristotle, God and the forms are not two but one. The forms are the ways in which God thinks, their dialectical structure is the articulation of His thought; and conversely. God is the activity whose diverse aspects we are describing whenever we identify this or that form. This identification of God with the forms removes all the objections brought by Aristotle against the Platonic theory of forms; for those objections are directed not against the conception of form as such—Aristotle himself constantly uses the conception—nor yet against the conception of transcendent forms existing apart from all matter—that, too, is a doctrine of his own no less than of Plato's—but against the conception of these forms as purely and simply objective, divorced from the activity of a thinking mind. Plato in the *Timaeus* represents God, in virtue of His creative act of will, as the efficient cause of nature, and the forms, in virtue of their static perfection, as its final cause; Aristotle, identifying God with the forms, conceives one single unmoved mover with a self-contained activity of its own, namely self-knowledge, νοήσεως νόησις, thinking the forms which are the categories of its own thought, and, since that activity is the highest and best possible (*Eth. Nic.* x. 7), inspiring the whole of nature with desire for it and a nisus towards reproducing it, everything in its degree and to the best of its power.

There are certain points in this theory which appear strange and even perhaps repulsive to persons brought up in a Christian tradition. In the first place, Aristotle has much to say about the love of God; but for him God does not love the world, it is the world that loves God. The love that makes the world go round is neither God's love for us nor our love for each other, but a universal love for God which is wholly unreciprocated. I do not want to explain away the contrast between this idea and those of Christianity, but I must point out that the contrast is diminished when we notice the difference of terminology. The word for 'love' in Aristotle is ἔρως, which means the longing of what is essentially imperfect for its own perfection; ἔρως is the upward-looking or aspiring love felt by that which feels itself inferior for that which it recognizes as its superior. That was explained once for all in the classical discussion of Ἔρως in Plato's *Symposium*. The Christian word for 'love' is ἀγάπη, which is originally the downward-looking or condescending love felt by a superior for an inferior; it is the contentment one has in things which though admittedly imperfect serve very well for the purposes of their station in one's life. By denying that God loves the world, Aristotle is only saying that God is already perfect and has in himself no source of change, no nisus towards anything better; by saying that the world loves God, he is saying that the world is restless in its search for a perfection already existing in God and identical with God.

But in the second place—and this is less easy to reconcile with our ordinary notions—Aristotle denies that God knows the world, and *a fortiori* denies that He created it by an act of will or has any providential plans for its history or the life of anything in it. Such a denial no doubt relieves the mind of many embarrassments; it relieves us of the necessity to think of God as beholding and tolerating, or still worse as deliberately causing, the evils of which the world is full, which is always a grave moral difficulty to the popular Christian theology; and it relieves us of the necessity to think of Him as seeing colours, hearing sounds, and so forth, which would imply His having eyes and ears, or alternatively as knowing a world so different from ours that we can no longer call it by the same name. But although these are great gains, they are offset by what we cannot but feel to be greater losses. The thought of God as watching over the life of the world, directing the course of its history, judging its actions, and bringing it ultimately back to unity with Himself, is a thought without which we can hardly care to think of God at all. Here again, I do not want to deny the contrast between the Aristotelian and Christian conceptions, or to suggest that the Aristotelian is, even on purely philosophical grounds, the better; but the contrast is mitigated if we recollect that the self-knowledge of God in Aristotle's theory means His knowledge of νοῦς as such, with its articulated structure of forms; and that since we too, so far as we are rational, share in νοῦς, our self-knowledge and our knowledge of the forms are participations by us in the life of God, and for that very reason bring us within the circle of God's self-knowledge. Even the blind impulses of inorganic nature, though in themselves neither parts of God nor known to God, are directed towards goals which *are* known to God and are indeed aspects of His nature.

§ 5. *Plurality of unmoved movers*

But it is necessary to get a little closer to the detail of Aristotle's cosmology, in order to show how he imagined the processes of nature to be produced by love of God. These processes are very complex; so complex, that one cannot regard them as all directed towards the same goal. We have already said that it was useless for Thales to say that both the magnet and the worm are simply water; that does not explain why one behaves like a magnet and the other like a worm. Now, if Aristotle is to explain the processes in the world by saying that everything is trying to imitate the life of God, that equally fails to explain the obvious differences between processes very different in kind and obviously directed towards the realization of very different ends. In other words, there must be a hierarchy of ends, and each order of beings must have an end of its own.

In order to meet this difficulty Aristotle devised a theory to the effect that the number of unmoved movers is not one but many. One of these is the first mover, namely God; its activity is pure self-thought, νόησις νοήσεως, and this absolutely self-contained and self-dependent activity of an immaterial agent is copied by an activity of a material agent (that is, a motion) which is as nearly self-contained and self-dependent as a motion can be, viz. a perfectly uniform rotation of the *primum mobile*, the outermost or stellar sphere of the heavens. The soul of the *primum mobile* is thus directly actuated by love of God, and moves its own body in a way as like the life of God as it is possible for a body's movement to be.

But the divine activity may be imitated in two ways: either by a body (which here as always in Greek cosmology means a living body, an organism endowed with soul and actuated by nisus, desire, or love) or by a disembodied mind or intelligence, νοῦς. God thinks or contemplates himself; other intelligences think or contemplate God. To that extent they share in the divine nature, but their participation in it is imperfect in so far as it is partial: each intelligence only apprehends part of the divine nature (that is, certain aspects of the intelligible world or world of forms) and hence each has a character and a mental life of its own, which is a peculiar mode or limitation of the character and life of God.

Now, according to Aristotle, there are cosmological reasons for believing in such intelligences. The uniform rotation of the *primum mobile* represents its endeavour to reproduce the unmoved activity of God; but the complex and erratic movement of a planet does not represent a wildly unsuccessful attempt to move uniformly in a circle, it represents a quite successful attempt to follow a rational and determinate path of a different and complicated kind. Greek geometry regards other curves as modifications of the circle, just as other grammatical cases are modifications of the nominative and other syllogistic figures modifications of the perfect figure, the first; and hence there must be some immaterial activity related to God's activity as the complex planetary path is related to the circle, and it is *this* immaterial activity, not that of God, which the soul of the planet is immediately symbolizing in material shape as a movement. The planetary path is an imitation of an imitation of God's activity, whereas the rotation of the *primum mobile* is a direct imitation of it in terms of body, and the thought of the planet's intelligence is a direct imitation of it in terms of intellect. The entire complex or society of intelligences form an immaterial and eternal model upon which the complex of cosmic movements is modelled: and here Aristotle is repeating in his own way the doctrine of the *Timaeus*, that in making the material or temporal world God modelled it upon an eternal pattern, viz. the immaterial or eternal world of forms. The idea common to both these doctrines is one of some importance, namely that the differentiation of activities which exists in the world of nature depends on a logically prior differentiation existing in eternal reality. Not only is immaterial being or absolute mind logically prior to nature, but the differentiation of mind into minds is prior to nature also.

Perhaps I may illustrate this point by referring to Sir David Ross's note on it in his edition of the *Metaphysics*, one of the very few points at which I am rash enough to differ from anything which he has said in that great work. He argues (i, p. cxl) that the intelligences are an illogical excrescence on Aristotle's theory: the celestial spheres, he says, ought to have been represented as celestial organisms striving each in its degree to reproduce the unchanging life of the one unmoved mover. But, I ask myself, what is meant by 'each in its degree'? Surely, it can only mean that a given celestial organism, say No. 35, is trying not simply to reproduce the activity of God, but to reproduce it in the special way appropriate to a body in the position of No. 35, very much as a right wing three-quarter is trying not simply to play football but to play it in the way appropriate to a right wing three-quarter. Hence, just as the idea or scheme of a Rugby XV is logically prior to the filling of each place by an actual player, so the idea or scheme of differentiated activities is prior to the movements of the actual spheres. In a word, Sir David Ross has conceded Aristotle's point by using that phrase 'each in its degree'.

§ 6. *Matter*

I must not linger over Aristotle, important though his cosmology is both in itself and as the form in which Greek thought concerning nature bequeathed its ripest heritage to the Middle Ages; but I cannot leave him without saying a word about his conception of matter. It is a very difficult thing to decide exactly what his theory of matter was, especially because, strangely enough, he has given no account of it in the fourth book of the *Metaphysics* which contains his lexicon of metaphysical terms. God, and in general mind, whether subjectively as that which thinks or objectively as the eternal objects or pure forms, contain no matter and cannot be embodied in matter; that which contains matter is that which is subject to the process of change, movement, or becoming. Now the matter in these things is in itself imperceptible and unknowable; sense perceives form only, but form incorporated in matter; intellect knows form only, and form not so incorporated. It is not to be expected, therefore, that Aristotle should give us a clear conception of matter; for him the phrase is a contradiction in terms, for that of which we can have clear conceptions is always form, and form is precisely not matter. What modern science calls the theory of matter, that is to say the theory of atoms, electrons, radiation, and so forth, is a description of various types of structures and rhythmical movements, and all this according to Greek terminology is a theory of form, not of matter at all, so that the Aristotelian agnosticism about matter contains nothing that need shock the modern physicist. In itself, matter is for Aristotle the indeterminate, that which might be but is not organized into this or that specific form or structure; hence he often identifies matter with potentiality, or that which is potentially either of two opposites, δύναμις τῶν ἐναντίων. When he tries to define it he can only do so negatively: 'By matter I mean that which in itself has neither quality nor quantity nor any of the other attributes by which being is determined' (*Met.* 1029ª20). Yet, although matter is unknowable and indescribable, it cannot be simply banished from cosmology, because it is the limiting case or vanishing-point at the negative end of the process of nature: everything in nature is constantly developing, that is, realizing itself or becoming in actuality what it always was potentially, and matter is the indeterminacy which is the negative aspect of potentiality. Thus a chick is trying to become a hen, but it is not yet a hen; there is in it a nisus towards the form of a hen, but there is also in it something in virtue of which that nisus has not yet reached its goal, and this something is what Aristotle calls matter. Matter is thus the unrealizedness of unrealized potentiality; and because there is no such thing as a wholly unrealized potentiality, a nisus that is altogether ineffective, there is no such thing as pure or mere matter; there is always and everywhere matter in process of organizing itself, matter acquiring form. But matter completely disappears only when form is fully realized and potentiality is resolved into actuality; hence Aristotle says that whatever is pure actuality contains no matter. Thus, anything situated somewhere in space is material, because it might be somewhere else and still remain itself; but there is nothing which God might be and is not, for the things which he is not, for example a stone, are things which he could not be without ceasing to be God; and hence God is pure actuality and contains no matter.

PART II

THE RENAISSANCE VIEW OF NATURE

I

THE SIXTEENTH AND SEVENTEENTH CENTURIES

§ 1. *Anti-Aristotelianism*

THE second great cosmological movement is that of the sixteenth and seventeenth centuries. Its leading characteristic may be seen most easily by considering it negatively, as a sustained polemic against the medieval thought inspired partly by Aristotle and partly by the philosophical views implicit in the Christian religion. The doctrine specially selected for attack was teleology, the theory of final causes, the attempt to explain nature as permeated by a tendency or endeavour to realize forms not yet existing. Typical of the whole movement is Bacon's celebrated gibe to the effect that teleology, like a virgin consecrated to God, produces no offspring—*tanquam virgo Deo consecrata, nihil parit* (*De Aug. Sci.* iii. 5). He meant that when an Aristotelian scientist accounted for the production of a certain effect by a certain cause by saying that the cause had a natural tendency to produce that effect, he was really telling you nothing at all, and was only distracting your mind from the proper task of science, namely the discovery of the precise structure or nature of the cause in question. The same criticism is implicit in Molière's ribald parody of an examination in the medical schools conducted in execrable dog-Latin according to Aristotelian methods:

Candidate: Mihi a docto doctore
          Domandatur causam et rationem quare
          Opium facit dormire.
          A quoi respondéo:
          Quia est in eo
          Vertus dormitiva,
          Cuius est natura
          Sensus assoupire.
Chorus of examiners:
          Bene bene bene respondere.
          Dignus, dignus est intrare
          In nostro docto corpóre.

In opposition to these teleological methods, the new theory of nature insisted on explanations through efficient causes, which meant explaining all change and process by the action of material things already existing at the commencement of the change. The assumption that change must be explained in this way is already a conscious principle in the philosophers of the sixteenth century. Thus Bernardino Telesio, in the middle of the century, regards nature not as drawn onwards by something outside itself to imitate forms having an eternal and immaterial existence, but as possessed of an intrinsic activity of its own, namely heat, in virtue of which it generates motion in itself and thus produces all the various types of structure found in the natural world. The naturalistic philosophy of the Renaissance regarded nature as something divine and self-creative; the active and passive sides of this one self-creative being they distinguished by distinguishing *natura naturata*, or the complex of natural changes and processes, from *natura naturans*, or the immanent force which animates and directs them. This conception was much closer to Plato than to Aristotle, for the tendency of Plato's Pythagorean cosmology was to explain the behaviour of natural things as an effect of their mathematical structure, a tendency quite in harmony with the work of the new physical science; whereas Aristotle's cosmology tended to explain it through an elaborate chain of imitations of imitations of the divine nature. Hence the Renaissance philosophers enrolled themselves under the banner of Plato against the Aristotelians, until Galileo, the true father of modern science, restated the Pythagorean-Platonic standpoint in his own words by proclaiming that the book of nature is a book written by God in the language of mathematics. For the Aristotelian doctrine that change is an expression of tendency, the sixteenth century substituted the Platonic doctrine—strictly the Pythagorean doctrine, for in essence it is pre-Socratic—that change is a function of structure.

§ 2. *Renaissance cosmology: First stage*

The theory of nature, in the sixteenth and seventeenth centuries, passes through two main stages. These are alike in their hostility to Aristotle and their rejection of teleology and insistence on the immanence in nature of formal and efficient causes; they are alike in a kind of neo-Platonism or neo-Pythagoreanism, I mean in their insistence on mathematical structure as the basis of qualitative differences. The difference between the two stages lies in their view of the relation between body and mind. In the early phase, the world of nature, which is now called *natura naturata*, is still conceived as a living organism, whose immanent energies and forces are vital and psychical in character. The naturalistic philosophies of the fifteenth and sixteenth centuries attributed to nature reason and sense, love and hate, pleasure and pain, and found in these faculties and passions the causes of natural process. So far their cosmology resembled that of Plato and Aristotle; and even more that of the pre-Socratics. But this animism or hylozoism was a recessive factor even in the early Renaissance cosmologies, whereas it had been a dominant one in Greek thought; as time went on it was submerged by the mathematical tendency which from the first had accompanied it; and as this tendency got the upper hand the idea of nature as an organism was replaced by the idea of nature as a machine. The change from the earlier or organic to the later or mechanical view was, as I shall explain, chiefly the work of Copernicus. But even the earlier view differed sharply from the Greek theory of the world as an organism, owing to its insistence on the conception of immanence. Formal and efficient causes were regarded as being *in* the world of nature instead of being (as they were for Aristotle) outside nature. This immanence lent a new dignity to the natural world itself. From an early date in the history of the movement it led people to think of nature as self-creative and in that sense divine, and therefore induced them to look at natural phenomena with a respectful, attentive, and observant eye; that is to say, it led to a habit of detailed and accurate observation, based on the postulate that everything in nature, however minute and apparently accidental, is permeated by rationality and therefore significant and valuable. The Aristotelian tradition, regarding nature as a material imitation of a transcendent immaterial model, implied that some things in nature were accidental. Aristotle himself had said that matter, i.e. the element of unintelligibility, was the source of the accidental element in nature; and it was not until the Aristotelian cosmology was swept clean away that scientists could begin to take nature seriously and, so to speak, treat her lightest word as deserving of attention and respect. This new attitude was firmly established by the time of Leonardo da Vinci at the end of the fifteenth century.

But at this early date nature was still regarded as a living organism, and the relation between nature and man was conceived in terms of astrology and magic; for man's mastery over nature was conceived not as the mastery of mind over mechanism but as the mastery of one soul over another soul, which implied magic; and the outermost or stellar sphere was still conceived in Aristotelian fashion as the purest and most eminently living or active or influential part of the cosmic organism, and therefore as the source of all events happening in the other parts; hence astrology. This magical and astrological conception had powerful enemies from the first, notably Pico della Mirandola, who attacked it in the late fifteenth century and was followed by several religious reformers such as Savonarola and Calvin; but in spite of this, the fifteenth and sixteenth centuries were predominantly given over to these occult sciences, which only died out by degrees, and died very hard, in the popular witchcraft of the seventeenth and eighteenth centuries.

§ 3. *Copernicus*

The crisis of modern cosmology dates to the middle of the sixteenth century. It was in 1543 that Copernicus's work on the solar system (*De revolutionibus orbium coelestium*) was posthumously published. The new astronomy expounded in this book displaced the earth from the centre of the world and explained the planetary movements on a heliocentric hypothesis. The philosophical significance of this new astronomy was profound, but it has often been misunderstood. It is commonly said that its effect was to diminish the importance of the earth in the scheme of things and to teach man that he is only a microscopic parasite on a small speck of cool matter revolving round one of the minor stars. This is an idea both philosophically foolish and historically false. Philosophically foolish, because no philosophical problem, whether connected with the universe, or with man, or with the relation between them, is at all affected by considering the relative amount of space they occupy: historically false, because the littleness of man in the world has always been a familiar theme of reflection. Boethius's *De Consolatione Philosophiae*, which has been called the most widely read book of the Middle Ages, contains the following words:

'Thou hast learnt from astronomical proofs that the whole earth compared with the universe is no greater than a point, that is, compared with the sphere of the heavens, it may be thought of as having no size at all. Then, of this tiny corner, it is only one-quarter that, according to Ptolemy, is habitable to living things. Take away from this quarter the seas, marshes, and other desert places, and the space left for man hardly even deserves the name of infinitesimal.' (Book ii, Prosa vii.)

Every educated European for a thousand years before Copernicus knew that passage, and Copernicus had no need to risk condemnation for heresy in order to repeat its substance.

The true significance of his astronomical discoveries was far more important. It consisted not so much in displacing the world's centre from the earth to the sun as in implicitly denying that the world has a centre at all. As his posthumous editor said, you could regard any point as its centre; and for the purpose of studying the planetary orbits it was convenient so to regard the sun. This statement has sometimes been regarded as due to timidity in the face of established doctrine, as if it amounted to saying 'I admit that the orthodox view is true, but the heliocentric view is nevertheless a convenient fiction'; but its real point was that the material world has no centre; and this was rightly regarded as a revolution in cosmology, because it destroyed the entire theory of the natural world as an organism. An organism implies differentiated organs; in the spherical world-organism of Greek thought there was earth in the middle, then water, then air, then fire, and lastly, for Aristotle, the *quinta essentia* of the world's outermost envelope; now, if the world has no centre, the very basis of these differentiations disappears; the whole world is made of the same kind of matter, the law of gravitation applies not only in the sublunary regions as Aristotle thought but everywhere, and the stars, instead of having a divine substance of their own, are homogeneous with our earth. This idea, so far from diminishing the scope of man's powers, vastly enlarged it; for it taught him that scientific laws established by him on earth would hold good throughout the starry heavens. It was directly owing to Copernicus's denial of geocentric astronomy that Newton could imagine the force which kept the moon in its orbit to be the same that drew his apple to the ground. For Aristotle, nature is made of substances differing in quality and acting heterogeneously: earth naturally moves towards the centre, fire away from the centre, and so forth. For the new cosmology there can be no natural differences of quality; there can only be one substance, qualitatively uniform throughout the world, and its only differences are therefore differences of quantity and of geometrical structure. This once more brings us back to something like Plato and the Pythagoreans, or again to something like the Greek atomists with their denial that anything is real except atoms and void and their reduction of all else to patterns of determinate atomic structure.

§ 4. Renaissance cosmology: Second stage. Giordano Bruno

Catholics and Protestants united to reject Copernicus's doctrines as heretical, and his immediate successors in astronomy (like Tycho Brahe, born three years after the publication of his book) refused to accept his system in its strictly astronomical bearing. But its philosophical importance, as I have explained, lay in the fact that its main thesis implied an homogeneity of substance between the earth and the heavenly bodies, and an identity in the laws governing their movements; and these implications were quickly welcomed by a new group of thinkers to whom belongs the credit of initiating the second and final stage in the Renaissance theory of nature. I will not here consider details concerning the personalities and doctrinal variations of the group, but will confine myself to its most important figure, that of Giordano Bruno.

Bruno, born in 1548, and becoming a Dominican friar early in life, was already obliged to leave Italy under an accusation of heresy before he was 30, and lived successively at Geneva, Toulouse, Paris, London, Wittemberg, and elsewhere; he returned to Italy to take up his residence at Venice under the protection of the Doge Giovanni Mocenigo, but was seized by the Inquisition there and tried at Rome over a period of seven years (1593–1600), and was finally burnt at the stake.

Bruno's most important contribution to the theory of nature

consisted in his philosophical interpretation of Copernicanism. He realized that the new astronomy, which he accepted with enthusiasm, implied a denial of any qualitative difference between terrestrial and celestial substance. He extended this denial, as Copernicus had never done, from the solar or planetary system to that of the fixed stars, admitting only one kind of distinction, namely that between fiery or luminous bodies and translucent or crystalline; all move according to the same laws, with an inherent circular motion, and the Aristotelian conceptions of natural heaviness and natural lightness are rejected. There is no first mover external to the material world; movement is intrinsic and natural to body as such. The material world is conceived as an infinite space, not empty but full of a yielding and plastic matter which recalls to our minds the ether of more modern physics; in this ether are innumerable worlds like ours, forming in their totality a universe not itself changing or moving but containing all change and movement within itself. This all-embracing and unchanging substance, the matrix of all change, is at once matter, in its capacity as extended and moving, and form or spirit or God, in its capacity as self-existent and the source of movement; but it is not a transcendent unmoved mover like the God of Aristotle but a mover immanent in its own body and causing movements throughout that body. Thus every particular thing and every particular movement has, in Bruno's language, both a principle, or a source within itself, and a cause, or source outside itself: God is both principle and cause, principle as immanent in each individual part of nature, cause as transcending each individual part.

This pantheistic cosmology reminds us on the one hand of the later Ionians, and on the other hand of Spinoza. It is like Anaximander in conceiving our world as one of an infinite number of vortices in an infinite homogeneous primary matter extending throughout infinite space, and in conceiving this matter as identical with God. And I must remark that just as the pantheism of Anaximander gave way, as Greek thought developed, to a doctrine according to which the world is not God but God's creature, so Bruno's pantheism gave way to a doctrine according to which the world is not divine but mechanical, implying therefore a transcendent God who designed and constructed it. The idea of nature as a machine is fatal to monism. A machine implies something outside itself. The identification of nature with God breaks down exactly when the organic view of nature disappears.

On the other hand, Bruno's thought resembles Spinoza's in so many ways that it has been described as stopping short of Spinoza's complete position only because Bruno was an unsystematic and desultory thinker, more rich in passion and intuition than in method and logical perseverance. But this is not the whole truth. Spinoza's cosmology presupposes the whole mechanistic theory of the universe, which Bruno's has not yet envisaged. The great feat of Spinoza is to bring together two conceptions which in Bruno are not yet distinguished, the conception of a world of mechanical matter and the conception of a world of mind, as these were worked out separately by Descartes.

Bruno's synthesis of the two ideas of principle and cause is only apparent. By principle he means immanent cause, *causa sui*: by cause he means transeunt cause, where A is the cause of B. In terms of pantheism, the world which is also God is, taken as a whole, the cause of itself; but the cause of any particular event is not the world as a whole but some other particular event. For the whole does not transcend this or that part of it; it is immanent in this or that part; what transcends any one part can only be another part. To speak of the whole as transcending a part is to degrade the whole to the status of one of its own parts. In order to clear up this confusion Bruno would have had to take one decisive step which he never took, viz. abandoning the conception of nature as an organism and developing the conception of nature as a machine.

§ 5. *Bacon*

Dualism is therefore not overcome in Bruno. It remains as a dualism between immanent and transcendent causation (causing oneself to move and being caused to move by something else). This was why in the seventeenth century there was a huge outbreak of dualisms: e.g. (*a*) in metaphysics, between body and mind; (*b*) in cosmology, between nature and God; (*c*) in epistemology, between rationalism and empiricism.

These dualisms emerge with Descartes. In Bacon (1561–1626)

they are not yet conscious. This can be seen from his account of
scientific method, where he sees no difficulty: he rejects both
empiricism and rationalism, comparing the empiricist to the
ant and the rationalist to the spider, whereas the true scientist
is like a bee, which transmutes what it wins from the flowers
into a new and precious substance: that is, the scientist advances
by means of experiments conducted in the light of theories and
uses them to test and confirm these theories. In his metaphysics Bacon followed the sixteenth-century tradition, and
regarded all qualitative differences in nature as functions of
structural differences which are ultimately quantitative in
character or amenable to mathematical study; thus he believed
firmly in the homogeneity or unity of substance; but his grasp
on the implications of this principle was very inadequate, and
he never realized the paramount importance of mathematics in
physical science. Hence, although it would be quite wrong to
identify him with the empiricist tendency in scientific method,
from which in theory he sharply dissociated himself, in practice
he constantly lapsed into it, substituting the classification of
qualitative differences for their explanation in quantitative
terms.

§ 6. *Gilbert and Kepler*

It was Gilbert's work on magnetism, published in 1600 and
rejected by Bacon, that determined the next step in the general
theory of nature. Gilbert, studying the force of magnetic attraction, suggested that attractive forces pervaded the whole of
nature and that all bodies exercised an attraction of this kind
upon all others. Kepler (1571–1630), early in the seventeenth
century, developed this suggestion with pregnant consequences.
By nature, he said, every body tends to remain stationary
wherever it happens to be—thus stating the principle of inertia
and emphatically repudiating the Greek and early Renaissance
conception of natural movements; but, he continued, whenever
one body is near another, its rest is disturbed by a mutual
affection which tends to draw every body towards its neighbour.
Thus a stone falls because the earth attracts it; and similarly,
Kepler suggested, the tides move because of the attraction of
the moon. With this clue to the phenomena of gravitation,
Kepler took the momentous step of proposing that in treating
of physics the word *anima* should be replaced by the word *vis*:

in other words, that the conception of a vital energy producing qualitative changes should be replaced by that of a mechanical energy, itself quantitative, and producing quantitative changes.

§ 7. *Galileo*

For Kepler this was a mere suggestion thrown out in a footnote; but for Galileo (1564–1642) it was a principle clearly grasped, with its presuppositions clearly stated.

'Philosophy', wrote Galileo, 'is written in that vast book which stands ever open before our eyes, I mean the universe; but it cannot be read until we have learnt the language and become familiar with the characters in which it is written. It is written in mathematical language, and the letters are triangles, circles and other geometrical figures, without which means it is humanly impossible to comprehend a single word.'[1]

The meaning is clear: the truth of nature consists in mathematical facts; what is real and intelligible in nature is that which is measurable and quantitative. Qualitative distinctions, like those between colours, sounds, and so forth, have no place in the structure of the natural world but are modifications produced in us by the operation of determinate natural bodies on our sense-organs. Here the doctrine of the mind-dependent or merely phenomenal character of secondary qualities, as taught by Locke, is already full-grown. English students of philosophy, finding this doctrine in Locke, do not always realize that it is by no means an invention of his, but had been long ago taught by Galileo as an important truth, and was in fact one of the leading principles of the whole scientific movement of the preceding two centuries; and that by the time it reaches Locke it is already somewhat out of date, and ready to collapse at the first touch of Berkeley's finger.

For Galileo, the secondary qualities are not merely functions of the primary and thus derivative and dependent on them, they are actually devoid of objective existence: they are mere appearances. Thus Galileo's world is 'a world of pure quantity, which through the inexplicable intrusion into it of living and sensible beings acquires the diversified qualitative aspect with which we are familiar'.[2] Nature, so regarded, stands on the one

---

[1] 'Il Saggiatore' (*Opere*, 1890, &c., vi, p. 232). Quoted in G. da Ruggiero, *La filosofia moderna*, i (Bari, 1933), p. 70.   [2] Ruggiero, op. cit., p. 74.

hand over against its creator, God, and on the other over against its knower, man. Both God and man are regarded by Galileo as transcending nature; and rightly, because if nature consists of mere quantity its apparent qualitative aspects must be conferred upon it from outside, namely by the human mind as transcending it; while if it is conceived no longer as a living organism but as inert matter, it cannot be regarded as self-creative but must have a cause other than itself.

§ 8. Mind and Matter. Materialism

With Galileo the modern science of nature reaches maturity. It was he who first laid down clearly and finally the terms on which nature could be an object of adequate and certain scientific knowledge. In a word, these terms were the exclusion of everything qualitative and the restriction of natural reality to a complex of quantities—quantities spatial or quantities temporal, but quantities and nothing more. The principle of science as understood by Galileo is that nothing is scientifically knowable except what is measurable.

I have indicated the steps by which this conception was reached; it remains to estimate the price paid for reaching it. First, nature is no longer an organism but a machine: that is to say, its changes and processes are produced and directed not by final causes but solely by efficient. They are not tendencies or efforts; they are not directed or orientated towards the realization of anything not yet existing; they are mere movements, produced by the action of bodies already existing, whether this action be in the nature of impact or in the nature of attraction or repulsion. Secondly, that which has been extruded from the concept of nature must find a lodgement somewhere else in metaphysical theory. These homeless entities fall into two main divisions: first, qualities in general; secondly, minds. According to Galileo, whose views on this subject were adopted by Descartes and Locke and became what may be called the orthodoxy of the seventeenth century, minds form a class of beings outside nature, and qualities are explained as appearances to minds: in Descartes's words they 'belong to the union of minds with bodies', and the senses by which we apprehend them are in general our organ for apprehending that union. This was the two-substance doctrine of mind and matter; but it was never held without strong opposition from a formidable minority. Descartes himself, the best philosophically equipped follower of Galileo, asserted this two-substance doctrine, but recognized that the two substances must have a common source, which he identified as God, and pointed out quite correctly that in that case the term 'substance' could be properly applied only to God: for if a substance is something existing in its own right, without the need of anything else (which is his definition of it), matter and mind, being created by God and therefore needing him in order to exist, are not strictly substances at all. They are only substances in a secondary sense of the word.

During Descartes's own lifetime, however, the pantheistic tendencies of the Renaissance were developed into a new direction. The idea of the world of nature as self-creative and self-regulating, combined with the idea of nature as a machine, gave rise to a materialistic theory of nature. The leader of this movement was the neo-Epicurean Gassendi, who held that the quantitative and mechanical nature described by Galileo was the only reality, and that mind was merely a peculiar kind of pattern or structure of material elements. This gave a monistic result which was metaphysically attractive; but it could never be worked out in detail, for no one could ever explain (far less demonstrate by experiment) what precise pattern of material elements produced either mind in general, or any particular kind of mental disposition or activity.

Materialism as the heir of Renaissance pantheism continued to live and thrive not only in the seventeenth century but throughout the eighteenth and even the nineteenth centuries, until it was finally destroyed by the new theory of matter which grew up in the late nineteenth century. To the very end it retained the impress of its pantheistic origin. This appears in the outspokenly religious character of its attitude towards the matter which it postulates as the only reality. It denies God, but only because it has transferred the attributes of God to matter, and being the offspring of a monotheistic tradition thinks one God quite enough. The phenomenon is so uniform that in a general way we can recognize a materialist author by his habit of using the traditional forms of Christian piety in speaking about the material world. On occasion he will even pray to it. Thus the famous materialist Holbach (Baron d'Holbach, 1723–89, a native of Hildesheim in Germany, but a writer of the most limpid and elegant French) closes his great work *Du système de la Nature* with what is nothing more nor less than a prayer to matter couched in such language that the alteration of a word here and there would lead any reader to think it an outpouring of Christian piety.

Scientifically speaking, on the other hand, materialism was from first to last an aspiration rather than an achievement. Its God was always a miracle-working God whose mysterious ways were past our finding out. The hope was always cherished that with the advance of science we should find them out some day; so the scientific credit of materialism was maintained by drawing very large cheques in its own favour on assets not yet to hand. Failing experimental confirmation in the laboratory—the kind of confirmation which was provided when biochemists achieved the feat of producing urea synthetically—a statement such as this, that the brain secretes thought in exactly the same way in which the gall-bladder secretes gall, might pass as a dogma of religion, but scientifically considered was simple bluff.

§ 9. *Spinoza*

Hence materialism, though it long continued to be a minority report, always remained on one side of the main tradition of European thought, a stagnant backwater of Renaissance ideas. The main stream moved from Descartes in another direction, namely that taken by Spinoza, Newton, Leibniz, and Locke. The idea common to all these was that matter was one thing and mind another and that both somehow proceeded from God as their source. God, as the source of all things, was regarded as working (so to speak) in two directions at once; in one direction he created the world of nature or matter; in the other direction he created the human mind, and whatever minds there may be besides.

This development was indicated plainly enough by Descartes himself; for, as I have said, Descartes did not advance a simple or unqualified two-substance doctrine; he qualified that doctrine by saying that because substance means that which exists of itself, or in its own right, there was strictly speaking only one substance, namely God.

Spinoza took this qualification seriously and drew its logical consequences. He asserted that there was only one substance, God; and that since there could be no other substance neither mind nor matter was a substance, and therefore neither mind nor matter was a substance created by God. Mind and matter, he said, were two 'attributes' of the one substance; and this one substance, after the fashion of Bruno but with far greater systematic coherence, he called indifferently God and Nature, representing it as an infinite unchanging whole which, *qua* extended, is the material world, and, *qua* thinking, is the world of mind. In both aspects it contains within it finite, changing, and perishable parts which are at once individual bodies and individual minds. Each part undergoes its changes solely through the operation of efficient causes, that is, through the action upon it of other parts; here Spinoza corrects Bruno, eliminating the last vestige of the early Renaissance hylozoism and, while accepting the physics of Galileo in its entirety, at the same time overcoming its main philosophical paradox, the separateness of material nature from the perceiving mind on the one hand and from its divine creator on the other, by insisting upon its inseparable unity with mind and giving to this unity the name of God. But in spite of the brilliant merits of Spinoza's cosmology—merits to which I cannot do justice in this brief description—it failed because the two attributes of extension and thought are held together in the theory, so to speak, by main force: there is no reason that Spinoza can give why that which is extended should also think, and vice versa; and consequently the theory remains at bottom unintelligible, a mere assertion of brute fact.

§ 10. *Newton*

But if Spinoza's theory of the relation between body and mind is at bottom unintelligible, it is obviously the work of an exceedingly intelligent mind which has understood the weak point of Descartes's theory and has worked heroically to amend it. This is more than can be said of Newton (1642–1727). Newton's work has placed him securely among the great thinkers; but when Wordsworth described his statue in Trinity as

The marble index of a mind for ever
Voyaging through strange seas of thought alone

he over-estimated not so much Newton's greatness as his loneliness and the strangeness of the ideas which he explored. In mathematics, it is true, he was an innovator and a notable one in discovering the differential calculus; but in this he was so far from being alone that the simultaneous and independent discovery of the same method by Leibniz gave rise to a squabble between the two great men which reflects ill on the moral character of both; and in any case the seeds of the discovery were obtained by each of them from a far more important invention, the analytical geometry of Descartes. The genius of Newton lay in the patient thoroughness with which he worked out the details of what he called, on the title-page of his immortal work, the 'Mathematical Principles of Natural Philosophy' (1687; ed. 2, 1713; ed. 3, 1726). But the main idea of that work is nothing more nor less than Descartes's idea of a 'universal science' mathematical in its form; the rules of method which he lays down at the beginning of his third book are drawn from Bacon; and the cosmology which he develops is nothing but Galileo's cosmology, according to which the natural world is a world of bodies possessing extension, figure, number, motion, and rest, modified by Kepler's idea of force and Gilbert's hypothesis of universal attraction between body and body: this natural world being regarded in the fashion of Galileo as a machine made by God and known by human beings who, in their capacity as sentient creatures, invest it with 'secondary qualities' of colour, sound, and so forth, which in its own right it does not possess.

Newton also owed something to the neo-Epicureans. Following them, he believed that all bodies consisted of minute particles surrounded by empty space. Their rest or motion in this empty space was determined, he thought, by forces of two kinds: *vis insita*, or inertia (an idea derived from Galileo), because of which they either rested or moved uniformly in a straight line; and *vis impressa*, which caused accelerated motions, and of which he recognized that there was more than one kind; he mentions two: (i) gravity or weight, which he defined mathematically as a force of mutual attraction varying directly as the product of the masses of the bodies concerned (where mass is defined as quantity of matter) and inversely as the square of the distance between their centres (where centre is circularly defined as centre of gravity); and (ii) electricity, of which he characteristically refuses to say anything on the ground that our experimental knowledge is at present inadequate.

Of the theoretical difficulties lurking among the foundations of his natural philosophy Newton seems quite unaware, although many of them had been familiar for a very long time. In the *Scholium* appended to his definitions he distinguishes absolute time, which 'in itself and without relation to anything external flows at a uniform rate', from relative time, which 'is measured by movement', without asking whether the two are really distinct, how anything can be said to 'flow' except relatively to something that stands still, or how it can be said to flow 'at a uniform rate' unless its flow is measured by movement. He distinguishes absolute space which 'is everywhere uniform and immobile', from relative space which 'is defined by our senses by its position relatively to bodies', again without asking any questions. He distinguishes absolute motion from relative motion, again in a quite uncritical way. And these uncritical distinctions form the groundwork of his entire treatise. To a critical eye they vanish as soon as they are looked at, leaving the conclusion, which Newton's successors have at last consciously embraced, that for what he called 'experimental philosophy' the only kind of time is relative time, the only kind of space relative space, and the only kind of motion relative motion.

Similarly, in the *Scholium Generale* at the end of the work he demolishes by unexceptionable arguments the Cartesian theory of vortices (that is, Descartes's view that the space vulgarly called empty is full of a continuous and very subtle matter in constant motion, which revolves in eddies round every body of gross matter, and that the rotary movement of a planet, for example, is caused by its floating in this subtle matter and being carried round in the solar vortex) and thinks that in this way he has demolished the doctrine that all space is full of matter and established the reality of empty space. He argues that since we cannot on his own principles explain why all the planets revolve in the same direction round the sun, or why their orbits are so disposed that they never bump into one another, this 'supremely elegant structure of the solar system cannot have arisen except by the device and power of an intelligent being', thus exalting the limitations of his own method into a proof of the existence of God. Finally, in the last paragraph of the whole work, as if to apologize for not having carried out the Cartesian programme of a universal mathematical science, he calls attention to some of the things he has left out. I will translate the whole paragraph.

'I should have liked to say something of the highly subtle spirit which pervades crass bodies and lurks in them, by whose force the particles of bodies attract each other to within minute distances and cohere in this contiguity; electrical bodies act at greater distances, repelling others as well as attracting them; light is emitted, is reflected, is refracted, is inflected, and warms bodies; and sensation is excited, and the limbs of animals are moved at will, by vibrations of this spirit propagated through the solid nerve-filaments from the external sense-organs to the brain and from the brain to the muscles. But these matters cannot be expounded in a few words; nor is there a sufficiency of the experiments by which the laws of this spirit's action would have to be accurately determined and demonstrated.'

There speaks a man great enough to be aware of his own work's shortcomings. He knows that his programme has been carried out only in part. But he is not great enough to be aware that the questions he has left unanswered bear upon those which he has answered. For example: are the phenomena of light consistent with his doctrine of empty space? Is the admission that a body coheres in virtue of a mutual attraction between its parts which is not gravitation, consistent with his doctrine that mass is simply quantity of matter? Is the admission that nature contains repulsive forces, as well as attractive ones, consistent with his doctrine that only an omnipotent God can prevent the planets from colliding with one another? And what reason has he for asserting that all the phenomena catalogued in this paragraph are due to one and the same *spiritus subtilissimus*?

Newton had become professor at the age of 27. He published the *Principia* at 43; from 54 to 85 he was controlling the Mint and living in the retirement of old age. One of the unsolved problems, mentioned in the paragraph I have quoted, we know that he tried to solve: that of light. He published the results in his *Optics* in 1704, at the age of 62; but he himself, as well as the friend to whom he submitted them for criticism, found them unsatisfactory. He had tried conclusions with that *spiritus subtilissimus*, and had suffered defeat. It is perhaps legitimate to infer that the careless and second-hand thinking on fundamental questions of cosmology, to which I have called attention, proved his undoing in the end.

§ 11. *Leibniz*

The cosmology of Leibniz is not unlike that of Spinoza in essentials, and in the last resort it breaks down over the same difficulty. For him, too, reality is both physical and mental, possessed both of extension and of thought; it consists of monads, each of which is a point spatially related to other points and also a mind apprehending its environment. The paradox of holding that every piece of matter has its mind is removed by the conception of low-grade mind; the conception, that is, of minds enormously more primitive and rudimentary than ours, whose perceptions and volitions are mere momentary flashes of mentality far below the threshold of consciousness. The great difference between Spinoza and Leibniz is that Leibniz emphatically reaffirms the doctrine of final causes; he has a clear conception of development and sees that development is nothing if it is not purposive, while at the same time he sees that if primitive mind is unconscious it can have purposes and yet be unconscious of them. Thus, Leibniz's nature is a vast organism whose parts are lesser organisms, permeated by life and growth and effort, and forming a continuous scale from almost unmitigated mechanism at one end to the highest conscious developments of mental life at the other, with a constant drive or nisus working upwards along the scale. Here again the theory has brilliant merits; but once more the relation between the mental and material aspects of reality is in the last resort unintelligible; for Leibniz saw, as Spinoza saw before him, that the life of an organism *qua* material, the physical process of nature, must be accounted for by purely physical laws, whereas its life *qua* mental must be accounted for solely by the laws of the mind; and hence, when he asks himself why a blow on my body should be accompanied by pain in my mind, he can give no answer except to say that there is a pre-established harmony between the two series of events, a harmony, that is, pre-established by the ordinance of God, the monad of monads. But by saying this Leibniz does not solve the problem, he only christens it with a long name.

§ 12. Summary: contrast between Greek and Renaissance cosmology

Before we take the next step let us pause to review the situation in which we stand. For the early Greeks quite simply, and with some qualification for all Greeks whatever, nature was a vast living organism, consisting of a material body spread out in space and permeated by movements in time; the whole body was endowed with life, so that all its movements were vital movements; and all these movements were purposive, directed by intellect. This living and thinking body was homogeneous throughout in the sense that it was all alive, all endowed with soul and with reason; it was non-homogeneous in the sense that different parts of it were made of different substances each having its own specialized qualitative nature and mode of acting. The problems which so profoundly exercise modern thought, the problem of the relation between dead matter and living matter, and the problem of the relation between matter and mind, did not exist. There was no dead matter, for no difference of principle was recognized between the seasonal rotation of the heavens and the seasonal growth and fall of leaves on a tree, or between the movements of a planet in the sky and the movements of a fish in the water; it was never for a moment suggested that the one could be accounted for by a kind of law which did not even begin to account for the other. And there was no problem of the relation between matter and mind, for no difference was recognized between the way in which an Athenian conceives and obeys the laws of Solon, or a Spartan the laws of Lycurgus, and the way in which inanimate objects conceive and obey those laws of nature to which they are subject. There was no material world devoid of mind, and no mental world devoid of materiality; matter was simply that of which everything was made, in itself formless and indeterminate, and mind was simply the activity by which everything apprehended the final cause of its own changes.

For the seventeenth century all this was changed. Science had discovered a material world in a quite special sense: a world of dead matter, infinite in extent and permeated by movement throughout, but utterly devoid of ultimate qualitative differences and moved by uniform and purely quantitative forces. The word 'matter' had acquired a new sense: it was no longer the formless stuff of which everything is made by the imposition upon it of form, it was the quantitatively organized totality of moving things. Now, this new idea of a material world was not a vain imagining; it had yielded solid results in the shape of physical science as that had been worked out by men like Galileo and Newton; and this new physical science was recognized on all hands as a genuine and secure possession of the human intellect, perhaps the greatest and most secure advance made by human knowledge since the Greeks invented mathematics. Just as Greek philosophy in the time of Plato had above all to take mathematics seriously, to recognize it as an established fact, and to ask not whether it was possible but how it was possible, so modern philosophy from the seventeenth century has been obliged as its first duty to take physics seriously, to confess that the knowledge acquired for mankind by Galileo and Newton and their successors down to Einstein is genuine knowledge, and to ask not whether this quantitative material world can be known but why it can be known.

I have indicated two ways in which this question was unsuccessfully answered in the course of the seventeenth century. One was materialism, or the attempt to explain knowledge as the specific activity of mind regarded as a special kind of material thing. This broke down because the modern conception of matter contained as its very essence the postulate that all activities of material things are describable in terms of quantity, as movements mathematically determined in time and space; and knowledge simply cannot be described in these terms. The other was the two-substance doctrine with its modifications in Spinoza and Leibniz, and this broke down because it was impossible to see any connexion between mind and matter as thus conceived. The corollary of such theories was their *reductio ad absurdum* in the view that mind could know nothing but its own states, and *ex hypothesi* the material world is not a state of mind.

II
THE EIGHTEENTH CENTURY

THE seventeenth century bequeathed unsolved to the eighteenth the problem of discovering some intrinsic connexion between matter and mind: some connexion which would preserve the special character of each, and yet make them genuinely and intelligibly parts of the same world. Two errors had to be avoided: first, their essential difference and indeed opposition must not be denied—mind must not be reduced to a special kind of matter, matter must not be reduced to a special form of mind; secondly, while this difference and opposition are still asserted, they must not be so asserted as to deny an essential unity connecting the two. By an 'essential' unity is meant a unity which is necessary to the existence of the things united. Thus, if a rope is stretched taut between two posts, there is a strain in one direction on one post and another strain, in the opposite direction, on the other. These are different strains; they work in opposite directions; and if the two posts are differently constructed and differently embedded in the ground, they will operate in very different ways; but there is an essential unity between them, because each strain is conditional upon the other.

§ 1. *Berkeley*

A solution of this problem was put forward by Berkeley. Accepting the seventeenth-century account of nature as a complex composed of inert matter—that is, matter whose every movement was produced by some *vis impressa*, the operation of some external efficient cause—a complex describable throughout in purely quantitative terms and wholly devoid of qualitative differences, he pointed out that this idea was an abstract idea, that is, the idea of something essentially incomplete, which must therefore be a partial account and not a complete account of the thing it professed to represent. In the language he inherited through Locke from Descartes and Galileo, the material world as described by the physicist possesses only primary qualities, but nature as we actually know it possesses secondary qualities too. Nowhere in nature do we find things having primary qualities without secondary; or, in more accurate language, nowhere do we find pure quantity devoid of quality. Quantity without quality is an abstraction, and a world of quantity without quality is an *ens rationis*, not a self-existing reality but a schematic view of certain selected aspects of reality. That is the first step in Berkeley's argument. The second step is this: the current doctrine, again inherited through Locke from Descartes and Galileo, attributes all qualitative differences in nature to the work of the mind. Colours exist because they are seen, and so forth. Now, if that is so, one integral element in nature as it actually exists is the work of the mind; and if nature as a whole cannot exist without that element, it follows that nature as a whole is the work of the mind.

Thus we get a wholly new metaphysical position. Taking the elements of the traditional seventeenth-century cosmology and simply rearranging them, Berkeley shows that, if substance means that which exists in its own right and depends on itself alone, only one substance need be asserted to exist, namely, mind. Nature as it exists empirically for our everyday perception is the work or creature of mind; nature in Galileo's sense, the purely quantitative material world of the physicist, is an abstraction from this, it is so to speak the skeleton or armature of the nature we perceive through our senses, and create in perceiving it. To sum up: we first, by the operation of our mental powers, create the warm, living, coloured, flesh-and-blood natural world which we know in our everyday experience; we then, by the operation of abstractive thinking, remove the flesh and blood from it and are left with the skeleton. This skeleton is the 'material world' of the physicist.

In the essence of Berkeley's argument as thus restated there is no flaw. He often expressed himself hastily, and often tried to support his contentions by argument that is far from sound; but no criticism of details touches his main position, and as soon as one understands the problem which confronted him one is bound to realize that he solved it in the only possible way. His conclusion may seem unconvincing, and the difficulties in which it places us are undeniable; but there is no way of escaping the admission that, if the conceptions of mind and matter are defined as they were defined by the cosmology of the seventeenth century, the problem of discovering an essential link between them can only be solved as Berkeley solved it. The emphasis of Berkeley's argument lies on the thesis that, matter being what by common consent it is, it can only be created in these two stages by a double operation of mind; but he left altogether untouched the complementary question, why, mind being what it is, should it perform this double operation and thereby create matter? This was the question asked by Kant in the section of the *Critique of Pure Reason* called the 'Transcendental Analytics'; and his answer was that if the current theory of mind is correct, that is to say, if the activity of thought has been correctly described by the logicians, the characteristics which physicists find to exist in the material world are precisely those which would exist in any object constructed for itself by the understanding; in other words, anyone who thought at all, provided he thought in the way described by logicians, would find himself constructing an object having the characteristics ascribed to matter by the physicists of the seventeenth century.

But there was another question which not only Berkeley but Kant himself left insufficiently treated. If nature is created by mind as the product of its thinking activity, *what* mind is it that thus creates nature? Obviously it is not the self-contained mind of this or that human individual. Neither Berkeley nor Kant nor any of their followers ever thought for a moment that Copernicus created the heliocentric planetary system, or Kepler its elliptical orbits, or Newton the inverse relation between the mutual attraction of two bodies and the square of the distance between their centres. Berkeley asserted quite definitely that the creator of the physical world was not any human or finite mind but an infinite or divine mind, God conceived as absolute subject or thinker. Thus he swept away the pantheism of the Renaissance thinkers, the theory of the physical or material world as God's body: which survived not only in the materialism that was still fashionable in his own day but even partially in Spinoza and Leibniz. For Berkeley, as for Plato and Aristotle and for Christian theology, God is pure thought and has no body; the world is not God but God's creature, something which He creates by His activity of thinking. But then arose the problem of the relation between God's infinite mind and the various finite human minds. For

Berkeley these are two quite different kinds of mind; God's mind becomes something like the *intellectus agens* of Aristotle which creates what it thinks, man's mind something like the passive intellect which passively apprehends an objective order given to it by God. But this was not really consistent with Berkeley's own starting-point; for when he inherited from Locke the doctrine that the mind creates one part at least of nature, the secondary qualities, this doctrine implied that the mind in question was human mind. Deny that, and the whole structure of Berkeleian idealism falls to the ground.

§ 2. *Kant*

Kant, more cautious and logical than Berkeley, insisted that the mind which makes nature is a purely human mind, *bloss menschliches*; but this again is not the mind of the individual human thinker but a transcendental ego, mentality as such or the pure understanding, which is immanent in all human thought (and it does not *create*, though it *makes* nature). Thus the Kantian form of idealism represents nature—by which I mean, as Kant meant, the physicist's nature, the material world of Galileo and Newton—as a product, not an arbitrary or irrational but an essentially rational and necessary product, of the human way of looking at things; and when we ask what these things are in themselves, Kant simply replies that we do not know.

The problem of the thing in itself is one of the most puzzling problems in Kant's philosophy. What makes it so puzzling is the fact that it seems impossible to state the problem without flatly contradicting yourself. The problem is stated in some such way as this:

Whatever we know, we know at once intuitively and discursively, that is, by the combined use of our senses and understanding. The only genuine intuition is sensuous intuition, and the only valid use of the understanding is to think about things which we sensuously perceive. The only knowledge, therefore, is an intelligent or thoughtful perception. Now, that which we perceive is made up (to use a modern term) of sense-data, and Kant accepted what for nearly two centuries had been the accepted view, that sense-data could exist only in relation to a sentient: they are essentially data, which therefore in order to exist must be given and received. Consequently, whatever we know is phenomenal only: that is, it exists only in relation to our knowing mind. So far this is consistent enough; but now comes the contradiction. The mind to which these data are given is not itself a datum; and that which gives it, the thing in itself, is not a datum either. The argument implies that there must be minds, and must be things in themselves; if these do not exist the whole argument falls to the ground; yet, since we can know only phenomena, we cannot on the argument know either minds or things in themselves. If so, how can we say that they exist? If the thing in itself is a mere synonym for the unknown, it is a nonsense phrase which makes nonsense of any argument into which it enters; and it does enter as an indispensable element into the whole structure of Kant's philosophy.

Kant's own attempt to get out of this difficulty often appears to his readers an addition of insult to injury. What he says is that although we cannot *know* the thing in itself we can *think* it: e.g. we think of it as that which gives us sense-data, and hence as something creative, and rationally creative; and since his ethical studies convinced him that a rational creative activity is to be found in the human will, he actually went so far as to suggest that the thing in itself is more like *will* than anything else. This brings him back to a metaphysics not very remote from that of Berkeley and Aristotle, a metaphysics according to which the ultimate ground of phenomena is to be sought in something which is at any rate more like mind than it is like matter. And it is Kant's opinion that whereas nature or the material world is known to us only as a collection of phenomena, owing their existence to our own thinking activities and essentially relative to these activities, our practical experience as active moral agents reveals to us not a mere collection of mental phenomena but mind as it is in itself. Any attempt (e.g. that made by psychologists) at a 'scientific' study of mind under laboratory conditions will result in the construction of 'mental phenomena' which are just as relative to our own modes of thinking as are the phenomena of nature. If we want to know what mind really is in itself, the answer is, 'Act, and you will find out'. In action we are, as we never are in scientific research, 'up against reality'. The life of action is a life in which the human mind achieves its own reality, its own existence as a mind, and at the same time achieves consciousness of its own reality as mind.

Hence, as Kant's critical philosophy develops, it seems to contradict itself at least twice. In the first critique (*Critique of Pure Reason*) where Kant is inquiring into the metaphysical foundations of physical science or knowledge of nature, his doctrine is that we can know only a phenomenal world which we make in the act of knowing it. In the second (*Critique of Practical Reason*), where he is inquiring into the metaphysical foundations of moral experience, his doctrine is that in moral experience we know our own minds as things in themselves. In the third (*Critique of Judgement*), his doctrine is that the thing in itself which underlies the phenomena of nature has the character of mind: so that what we know in our practical or moral experience is of the same kind as what we think, but cannot know, in our theoretical experience as students of natural science.

The ordinary modern reader ignores this side of Kant's philosophy, because it seems an insult to his intelligence to take seriously a doctrine which in one breath tells him that the thing in itself is unknowable and claims to tell him what it is. But this is to misunderstand Kant. Kant never for a moment thought that the thing in itself was unknowable in the sense in which his critics understand that statement. The words *wissen*, *Wissenschaft* in Kant have the same kind of special or restricted significance that the word 'science' has in ordinary modern English. Science is not the same as knowledge in general; it is a special kind or form of knowledge whose proper object is nature and whose proper method of procedure is exactly that combination of perception with thought, sensation with understanding, which Kant has tried to describe in the *Aesthetics* and *Analytics* of the *Critique of Pure Reason*. Kant has not given us a theory of knowledge in the modern sense of the term: what he has given us is a theory of *scientific* knowledge; and when he said that we could think the thing in itself though we could not know it he meant that we had knowledge of it but not scientific knowledge.

And in this connexion I may remark that the attempt to mark out a special field for scientific knowledge, outside which there should lie other fields to be explored by other forms of thought, was not new. Descartes's project of a universal science was explicitly conceived as leaving outside itself the three great fields of history, poetry, and divinity. The forms of thought which held good in these fields were not regarded by Descartes as invalid or worthless; we have no right to doubt his sincerity when he tells us that he attaches high importance to them; but he regards them as fields in which his proposed method, just because it is in the narrow sense a scientific method, will not apply. Kant inherited this point of view from Descartes, and differed from him chiefly in the one point that, whereas Descartes placed metaphysics inside the proper sphere of scientific method, Kant placed it outside.

Kant's view, then, comes to this: the proper *object* of scientific knowledge is not God or mind or things in themselves, but nature; the proper *method* of scientific knowledge is a combination of sensation with understanding; and since nature is that which we know by this method, it follows that nature is mere phenomenon, a world of things as they appear to us, scientifically knowable because their ways of appearing are perfectly regular and predictable, but existing only in so far as we take up the point of view from which things have that appearance. These truths are known to us by a kind of knowledge that is not scientific: let us call it philosophical. Our knowledge that there are things in themselves, then, is philosophical knowledge, and this is the kind of knowledge that must teach us what things in themselves are.

If we try to find out exactly how Kant did think of the thing in itself, in other words what his philosophical doctrine of it was, we can get no clear answer. There are two possible explanations of this fact. In general, if someone does not say something the reason may be either that he cannot make up his mind about it and has nothing definite to say, or that he thinks it so obvious that it does not need saying. It might be that Kant was so much under the influence of the metaphysical scepticism of writers like Voltaire and Hume that he really doubted whether there could be a philosophical theory of the thing in itself, although the logic of his own position implied the possibility of such a theory. Or again, it might be that he was still so far influenced by his early training in the school of Leibniz that he took it for granted that the thing in itself was mind. Perhaps both explanations contain part of the truth and are not incompatible. The first awakening from a dogmatic slumber into a state of scepticism brings one into a condition not very far removed from dogmatism itself. This at any rate is clear, whatever the reasons for it may have been, that Kant, while rightly insisting that the idea of a thing in itself was an essential element in his philosophy (for he gave that definite answer when challenged on the point in his old age by Fichte), never took in hand the task of working out that idea and saying to himself, 'since I admit that we can and do think the thing in itself I must make up my mind exactly *how* we think it and what we think it is'.

By neglecting to do this, Kant imposed on his successors the task of doing it for him. Fichte tried to solve the problem by cutting it out, eliminating the thing in itself and representing the mind as constructing nature out of nothing. This produced a philosophy which on the face of it looked like a Kantianism made for the first time coherent and logical; but it really destroyed the Kantian problem instead of solving it, for the problem arises not from a general consideration of knowledge but from the special peculiarities of nature as something *given* to mind, something with which mind finds itself confronted, and this implies that there is a thing in itself. The alternative method of developing Kant was therefore the right one, and this was adopted by Hegel.

HEGEL: THE TRANSITION TO THE MODERN VIEW OF NATURE

KANT admitted that we can and may think of the thing in itself; but he set his followers the task of discovering how in fact we must and do think of it.

The person who set himself this task as the starting-point of all cosmological theory was Hegel. Rejecting the exclusive claim of scientific thought to the title of knowledge, and consequently rejecting the idea that the thing in itself is unknowable, he affirmed that the thing in itself is the easiest of all things to know: it is simply pure being, being as such, without any particular determinations whether qualitative or quantitative, spatial or temporal, material or spiritual. The only reason why it seems to be unknowable is because there is nothing particular in it to know; it has no characteristics to distinguish it from anything else, and so when we try to describe it we fail, not because we cannot understand the mystery of its nature but because we understand perfectly well that there is nothing there to describe. Being in general is nothing in particular; so the concept of pure being passes over, as Hegel puts it, into the concept of nothing. This passage or logical transition from one concept to another is not a merely subjective or psychological transition of our thought from one concept to a different concept; it is an objective transition, a real process by which one concept evolves itself logically out of another which it presupposes. This is the idea of becoming, development or process, which in its primary or fundamental form is logical becoming: a process, but not a process in time or a movement in space, still less a change of mind or process of thought, but a process of the notion, a logical movement inherent in concepts as such. Thus Hegel has answered the question how the thing in itself can be creative or a source of something other than itself: its activity is the same as what we call logical necessity, the inherent power by which one concept generates another, which is at once a fresh concept and a new form of itself. The concept grows like an organism, passing from potentiality to actuality by sprouting new determinations of itself which are heterogeneous with their undifferentiated starting-point.

From this beginning Hegel develops a system of concepts which he expounds in what he calls the science of logic. This system of concepts is like the Platonic world of forms in being immaterial, purely intelligible, organically constructed, and the presupposition of all material and mental existence. The difference between Hegel's conception and Plato's is that whereas Plato's world of forms is static, devoid of change and becoming, Hegel's is permeated through and through by process, it is dynamic, its being constantly issues in a becoming where every concept leads on by logical necessity to the next. This overcomes Aristotle's objection to Plato that his forms, because they are static, cannot explain the origin of change and process in the natural world; for Hegel, the changes in nature and indeed the origin of nature are an outcome or logical consequence of the process in the world of concepts: logical priority is the ground of temporal priority. Hence, unlike Aristotle, Hegel need not place a thinker or mind at the beginning of his cosmology as the first cause; it is true that he describes God as the object which the science of logic studies, but God is not for him a mind—that is a falsely anthropomorphic way of conceiving Him; God is the self-creating and self-subsisting world or organism of pure concepts, and mind is only one, though the highest and most perfect, of the determinations which God acquires in that process of self-creation which is also the process of creating the world. Here lies Hegel's answer to the problem of the relation between human mind and divine mind, which Berkeley left unsolved and Kant gave up as insoluble: the importance of man in the world lies precisely in the fact that he is the vehicle of mind, the form in which God's being or rather becoming develops itself into its crowning phase as the being or becoming of spirit. This resembles pantheism in that the process of the world is conceived as identical with the process of God's self-creative life; but it differs from pantheism in that God in Himself, as the pure creative concept, is prior to the material world and transcends it as its cause.

This dynamic world of forms, which Hegel refers to collectively as the Idea, is the source or creator immediately of nature and mediately, through nature, of mind. Thus Hegel rejects the subjective idealism, as he calls it, of Berkeley and Kant, according to which mind is the presupposition or creator of nature; that, says Hegel, inverts the relation between them, and he prefers in this respect the materialistic view of nature as the source of mind. In his eyes the only error of that view is to make nature something absolute, self-creative or self-explanatory, whereas in point of fact, he thinks, the subjective idealists are right, as were Plato and Aristotle, in regarding nature as essentially created, derivative, dependent upon something else: only that something else is for him not mind but the Idea. And Hegel thoroughly agrees with Plato in regarding the Idea not as a state of mind, or an activity of mind, or a creature of mind, not in short as anything subjective, but as a self-contained and self-existing realm of being which is the appropriate object of mind. This is what Hegel calls 'objective idealism', as opposed to the subjective idealism of Kant, or alternatively 'absolute idealism' because it conceives the Idea as something real in itself and not depending in any way upon the mind that thinks it.

I am here following Hegel in describing the philosophical view common to Kant and Berkeley as subjective idealism. I am not sure whether Hegel invented the name, but in any case our ordinary use of it comes from him and consequently he has a right to be consulted as to its meaning. As he used it, subjective idealism is the theory that ideas or concepts exist only for a subject, or (as Hegel puts it) the illusion that 'ideas exist only in our heads'. He regards this illusion as a legacy of the Cartesian body-mind dualism, which has trained people to think that whatever is not material is mental, so that the concept, instead of being a presupposition of thought, is twisted into a mere way of thinking, an act or habit of thought. Subjective idealism in this sense must be clearly distinguished from solipsism, which is the theory—actually held by one school of Cartesians—that nothing exists except myself, i.e. my mind. That, of course, is one form of subjective idealism, but not a form ever held either by Berkeley or by Kant.

Hegel's philosophy is a system in three parts. The first part is logic, or the theory of the Idea. The second part is the theory of nature; the third is the theory of mind. These three together form what he calls the encyclopaedia of the philosophical sciences, and every philosophical topic and doctrine falls

somewhere into a place in this framework. I shall of course make
no attempt here to give an account of the system as a whole; I
shall merely try to outline Hegel's conception of nature and to
show how it stands to the Idea on the one hand and to mind on
the other.

Nature, for Hegel, is real; it is in no sense an illusion, or
something which we think to exist when what really exists is
something else; nor is it in any sense a mere appearance, something which only exists because we think it. It really exists,
and exists independently of any mind whatever. But the word
'real' is somewhat ambiguous. Literally, it means having the
character of a *res* or thing; and if things are what exist in space
and time, nature is not only real but it is the only reality, for
it is precisely the totality of things, the realm of thinghood.
But in ordinary usage the word 'real' has at least one other
meaning: as when we say that this picture is not a real Rem-
brandt but only a copy. The picture is a thing, it has *realitas*;
but it has not *veritas*; it does not embody the idea which it
professes to embody.

Now, according to Plato and Aristotle, all natural things are
essentially things engaged in a process of becoming; and this is
because they are always trying to become adequate embodi-
ments of their own forms and never quite succeeding. In this
sense everything in nature is to some extent unreal in the
second sense of the word: not a mere appearance, still less an
illusion, but something not altogether succeeding in being itself.
Hegel accepts this Platonic-Aristotelian view of nature.

Nature is permeated, for Hegel as for Aristotle, by nisus;
everything in nature is trying to become something definite; but
the convergence of the process upon its own proper goal is
always asymptotic and never reaches the point of coincidence.
This is why the laws of nature are what modern scientists call
statistical laws, not describing with rigid accuracy the behaviour
of each single individual to which they apply, but describing
the general tendency of their behaviour, the type of behaviour
towards which their movement is orientated. In this sense
nature is not real; nothing in nature fully and completely tallies
with our scientific description of it; and this not because our
descriptions are in need of correction, but because there is
always in nature a certain backlash, an element of indeter-

minacy, of potentiality (to use Aristotle's language) not yet
resolved into perfect actuality.

What is the reason for this element of backlash or indeterminacy in nature ? Hegel's answer to this question is profoundly
original. The Greeks had been inclined to throw the blame for
it upon matter, and to suggest that the form, though perfect in
itself, was not perfectly embodied in matter because the matter
was somehow recalcitrant ; but this was no answer, because the
alleged recalcitrance of matter was only a name for the fact that
the form, for whatever reason, was not perfectly embodied
there. Hegel's view is that the forms of nature fail to get
perfectly embodied because of a certain peculiarity in these
forms themselves. They are forms of a peculiar kind, which
owing to something in their very structure cannot be completely
realized. The task which nature sets herself in trying to realize
them is therefore an inherently impossible one, and can only be
accomplished in an imperfect and approximate way. They are,
so to speak, Utopian forms, at once demanding realization and
yet having in them something which makes realization impossible. What makes their realization impossible is the fact
that they are 'abstract': that is, the fact that they stand over
against their own instances as transcendent patterns which in
themselves are essentially immaterial but which nevertheless
demand to be reproduced in matter.

The concepts of nature may be contrasted in this respect with
two other types of concept: those of pure logic and those of
mind. The concepts of pure logic are determinations of pure
being, and all belong as necessary attributes to anything whatever; there is no possibility of anything's failing to exhibit
any one of them, because they are all bound up together in such
a way that where one of them is realized all are realized; and
they are all realized everywhere. The description of them is the
elaborated or developed description of anything whatever just
so far as it is anything—a body or a mind or anything else, if
there is anything else.

The concepts of mind, on the other hand, are (like those of
nature) concepts determining the character of a special kind of
actually existing thing: but this thing (viz. the mind) has the
peculiarity that it imposes this character upon itself by its own
free activity, and therefore is free to develop in itself a perfect

possession of this character. They define what mind ought to be, and what mind ought to be it can be, and indeed only knows that it ought to be this in so far as it is already being this. Morality, e.g., is a concept of mind; and only a mind which is already a moral agent recognizes that it ought to be a moral agent.

The way in which Hegel thinks of the concepts or forms which direct the processes of *nature* is parallel to the way in which Plato thought of *all* forms. For instance, Plato himself explains that the conception of the ideal State cannot be exactly realized in any actual State, because human nature, being what it is, can never organize itself into a perfect embodiment of that conception; yet the demand that this shall be done, the demand that the form of the ideal State shall be realized in human nature, is a demand essential to the form itself: so that the form sets human nature a task which it cannot shirk and yet can never hope really to accomplish.

But why should Hegel have supposed that all the forms of nature have this curious character? For answer, we must ask what is the differentia of nature, the peculiarity which distinguishes it as a whole from the Idea on the one hand and from mind on the other. Hegel's answer is that nature is essentially reality as external, the external world. Here external does not mean external *to us*. Nature is in no sense external to us. It is not external to our bodies; on the contrary our bodies are part and parcel of it; nor is it external to our minds, for no one thing can be outside another unless both occupy positions in space and are therefore material bodies; and our minds, not being bodies, are not situated anywhere in space; indeed, if they were, they too would be parts of nature. What is meant by calling nature the external world is that it is a world pervaded and characterized by externality, a world in which everything is external to everything else. Nature, then, is the realm of outwardness; it is a world (or rather *the* world) in which things are outside each other. This outwardness has two forms: one in which every thing is outside every other thing, namely space; the other in which one thing is outside itself, namely time. When I say that a thing is outside itself in time, I mean that the realization of its concept or idea is spread out over time; the various elements which go to make up that concept, the various attributes or characteristics of the thing, are separated from each other by belonging to it successively, and cannot belong to it together. It is in the nature of a heart, for example, that it should both expand and contract; but because the process involving these two phases is a natural and not a logical one, the transition from one phase to the other takes place in time, and the heart stops doing one thing when it begins doing the other. Its complete being, as a heart, involves both systole and diastole; but this being is broken up and realized piecemeal, time being the manner of its breaking-up and of its piecemeal realization.

The idea of nature, according to Hegel, is the idea of a reality thus doubly broken up, spread out or distributed over space and time. This characteristic affects not only the idea of nature as a whole, but every idea of any thing in nature. The idea of a material body is the idea of a number of particles distributed in space; the idea of life is the idea of a number of characteristics distributed in time. Hence there is no one place at which the idea of a body can be locally exemplified, and no one time at which all the characteristics of life can be actualized. You can nowhere say, the body is *here*; you can never say, I am *now*, at this instant, alive. Even if you indicate a cubic foot of space when you say *here*, and a span of eighty years when you say *now*, you still cannot say that the being of the body is wholly contained within that region, or the being of the organism within those eighty years; in both cases the being of the thing overflows beyond these boundaries; the body makes itself felt by its gravitational effects throughout space, and the organism, whether you look at it physically, chemically, biologically, or morally, is only a temporal and local concretion in a life-stream stretching vastly beyond it on all sides, and what we call its peculiarities are really characteristics pervading that life-stream as a whole.

Following this line of thought we soon arrive at the conception, which Whitehead has rediscovered and made familiar in our own time, that each piece of matter in the world is located not *here* or *there* simply, but everywhere. This conception, as Whitehead has well insisted, is by no means shocking to modern physics; and this is a remarkable fact about modern cosmology, that the physical science of to-day has arrived at a view of matter and energy which so far agrees with the implications of

Hegel's theory of nature, that a philosopher-scientist like White-head can restate Hegel's theory (not knowing that it is Hegel's, for he does not appear to have read Hegel, so far as I can judge) and allow that theory to take him wherever it likes, setting his sails to it with a good conscience and cheerfully resolving the concept of nature, as he says himself, into the concept of pure activity. What is possible for Whitehead, however, was not possible for Hegel, because the physics of Hegel's day was still the physics of Galileo and Newton, a physics conceived in terms of things 'simply located' (to use Whitehead's term) in space. Consequently the whole Hegelian theory of nature is rent by a dualism which in the long run breaks it in pieces. On the one hand there is the presupposition which he inherited from the seventeenth century, the conception of nature as a machine, a moving congeries of pieces of dead matter; on the other hand there is the cosmological implication of his own thought, which insists that all reality must be permeated by process and activity; that nature cannot be a mere machine, because it has in it the power to evolve out of itself, by a logical necessity, life and mind.

Hegel belonged to a generation of Germans who worshipped ancient Greece with an almost idolatrous worship and studied its art, literature, and thought with passionate intensity. The organicism or anti-mechanism of Hegel's *Naturphilosophie* might be cheaply and easily described as a philosophy in which the unsolved problems of eighteenth-century thought were solved by borrowing from the thought of ancient Greece. I say cheaply and easily, because these methods of description are charac-teristic of that frivolous and superficial type of history which speaks of 'influences' and 'borrowings' and so forth, and when it says that A is influenced by B or that A borrows from B never asks itself what there was in A that laid it open to B's influence, or what there was in A which made it capable of borrowing from B. An historian of thought who is not content with these cheap and easy formulae will not see Hegel as filling up the chinks in eighteenth-century thought with putty taken from Plato and Aristotle. He will see Hegel as the point at which, through its own spontaneous development, eighteenth-century thought became sufficiently mature to understand Plato and Aristotle and therefore to connect its own problems with the problems which it found them discussing. But in making this contact with Greek ideas Hegel lost contact with the practical life of his own generation. Hegel was a revolutionary. His view of nature led (consciously) to revolutionary conclusions about the correct procedure of scientific research. He wanted to go from Galileo more or less direct to Einstein. But he lived in a generation of counter-revolutionaries who maintained that what was good enough for Newton was good enough for them and would be good enough for all future generations. This quarrel between Hegel and his contemporaries arose from certain discrepancies in Hegel's own thought.

He followed Kant and Newton, Descartes and Galileo, in taking empty space and time as the fundamental things in nature, the double framework over which all natural fact is spread out; the movement which pervades nature he takes, in the Platonic-Aristotelian manner, as a translation of something more fundamental, namely, logical process, into terms of space and time; but he sees that if the conception of nature as thus spread out over space and time is taken seriously, it leads to the conclusion that no natural thing or process ever has a home of its own either in space or in time, and consequently the very idea of existing in space or happening in time is an idea that contradicts itself.

In this situation, what is Hegel to do? Some philosophers, when they find a thing to contain self-contradictions, argue that therefore it is only an appearance, not a reality. But that method of escape is not open to Hegel, because he is an ultra-realist in his theory of knowledge, and thinks that whatever appears, so long as it really does appear, is real. Now, nature really does appear to us; it is visibly present to our senses, or rather, as Kant had shown, not to our senses but to our imagination, and intelligibly present to the thought of the scientist. It is therefore real. But the contradiction in it, according to Hegel, proves that it is not complete; it is something which is engaged in turning into something else. This other thing, into which nature is turning, is mind. We may therefore say if we like that for Hegel nature implies mind. But this implication has nothing to do with any train of thinking. It does not mean that when we think of nature we are obliged to go on and think of mind. Nor does it mean that nature is something which cannot exist unless mind exists too. It means that nature is one phase in a real process which is leading on to the existence of mind. Nature for him is an abstraction, as it is for Berkeley and Kant; but a real abstraction, not a mental abstraction. By a real abstraction I mean a real phase in a real process, in itself, and apart from the subsequent phase to which it is leading. Thus, the growth of a leaf-bud is a process which really happens, and happens before the leaf is fully formed; the separateness of the two things, bud and leaf, is not a fiction of the human mind; but although the bud has a character of its own really different from that of the leaf, it is also engaged in turning into a leaf, and this activity of turning into a leaf is part of its essence, indeed it is the most essential part of that essence. Bud and leaf are thus phases of one process, and the bud in itself is an abstraction from that process, but an abstraction made by nature, which everywhere works in this way through successive phases of the process, doing one thing before it goes on to the next. Now, for Hegel nature as a whole implies mind in the same way in which the bud implies the leaf; nature must first of all be itself, so our conception of it is true and not illusory; but it is only being itself provisionally; it is going to stop being itself and turn into mind, as the bud is only being itself in order to stop being a bud and turn into a leaf. And this provisional character of the bud as a transitory phase in the whole process appears logically as a self-contradiction in the idea of a bud, a contradiction between what it is being and what it is becoming. The contradiction is no fault of the botanist's; it is not a fault at all; it is a characteristic inherent in reality so far as reality means what exists here and now, that is, the world of nature.

In one respect the parallel between the process from bud to leaf and the process from nature to mind is imperfect. The process from bud to leaf is a process within nature and is therefore in time: the bud exists at one time and the leaf at a later time. Obviously the transition from nature to mind cannot fall within nature, for it takes us beyond the idea of nature; therefore the transition is not a temporal transition but an ideal or logical one. There will never be a time, according to Hegel, when all nature will have turned into mind, and conversely there never was a time when none of nature had turned into mind; mind always is and always has been growing out of nature, somewhat as gravitating bodies have always been generating fields of force, or as the series of numbers has always been generating itself to infinity.

This brings us to a point where Hegel's cosmology differs sharply from most of those current to-day: it is indeed the main or crucial point of difference. The point to which I refer is concerned with the significance of time. Modern cosmologies are in general based on the idea of evolution, and represent the development not only of one natural species or order as a development in time, but also the development of mind from nature as a development in time. Views of this kind were already being canvassed in Hegel's day, and he considered them, only to reject them with emphasis. All reality, he says, is a system of strata or grades, higher and lower; this is true both of mind, where there is a lower stratum of sense and a higher one of intellect, with subdivisions, and also of nature, where the inorganic or lifeless and the organic or living are the two main divisions; and in nature, which is the realm of externality, the living and the lifeless instead of interpenetrating must exist outside one another as separate classes of things. But he insists that there cannot be a temporal transition, but only a logical transition, from the lower forms in nature to the higher. Now, there is a reason why Hegel took up this position. The reason is, that a purely dead and mechanical world of matter, as conceived by the physics of his day (which he accepted as his starting-point), cannot conceivably produce life by doing the only thing which it has the power to do, namely, redistributing itself in space. There is a new principle of organization at work in living things, which differs qualitatively from that of dead matter; and since the realm of matter was *ex hypothesi* devoid of qualitative differences, it could not produce that particular qualitative novelty in itself. Consequently, so long as physicists were content with their conception of dead matter, their authority made it impossible to accept a theory of evolution.

Here once more we observe the incompleteness of Hegel's *Naturphilosophie*, the unremoved contradictions in its logical basis. What was he doing? Was he trying to give a philosophical account in the Kantian manner, of what natural scientists had actually done and did actually believe? In other words, is his *Naturphilosophie* an attempt to answer the question *how* natural scientists come to know what they do in fact know? Or was he trying to go behind the results already achieved by natural scientists and to get a different set of results by a method which was not the traditional method of natural science but his own philosophical method?

He has been blamed for doing both these things, each time on the ground that he ought to have been doing the other. The fact is that he really was doing both. He begins by provisionally accepting natural science as it stood in his own day (and he has been frequently and bitterly and very unfairly blamed for doing that, in other words for accepting what was told him by men who, because they lived in the late eighteenth century, are by now supposed to be mere examples of medieval folly), and he goes on to find himself deeply dissatisfied with this contemporary natural science and trying to improve on it according to his own ideas of what science should be. And he has been frequently and bitterly and very unfairly blamed for that too, in other words for *not* accepting what these same alleged fools told him, and for trying to criticize their work when he ought to have left it alone as 'scientific' and therefore sacrosanct.

Hegel was struggling to bring about a synthesis between contemporary science and the results he had achieved by his own methods, between the conception of nature as a machine and the conception of all reality as permeated by process. He was right in thinking that a synthesis was needed. I do not say that he was right with regard to the particular synthesis at which he arrived. What I say is that he was in a hurry, and tried (having committed himself to an unsatisfactory distinction between natural science and philosophy) to solve by philosophy the problems of natural science, not seeing that natural science must solve its own problems in its own time and by its own methods. He tried to anticipate by philosophy something which in fact could only be a future development of natural science. His anticipation, as we can now see, was in many ways startlingly accurate; but scientific thought has no place for anticipation; it only values results scientifically achieved.

PART III

THE MODERN VIEW OF NATURE

I

THE CONCEPT OF LIFE

§ 1. *Evolutionary biology*

SINCE Hegel's day the concept of evolution has passed through two main phases: first, a biological phase; then a cosmological.

The biological phase is of extreme importance in its relation to the general theory of nature, because it was this movement of thought which ultimately broke down the old Cartesian dualism of matter and mind by introducing between them a third term, namely, life. The scientific work of the nineteenth century was largely devoted to establishing the autonomy of the biological sciences as forming a separate realm, independent of physics or the science of matter on the one hand and the science of mind on the other. In ancient and medieval cosmology the ideas of matter, life, and mind were so fused together as to be hardly distinguishable; the world, *qua* extended, was regarded as material; *qua* moving, as alive; *qua* orderly, as intelligent. The thought of the sixteenth and seventeenth centuries expelled its soul from the world, and created modern physics by conceiving the orderly movements of matter as dead movements. There was already implicit in this conception a contrast with living movements, but modern biology was as yet unborn, and Descartes deliberately tried to think of animals as automata, that is, to explain biological facts in terms of the new physics. Even in Hegel, the division of his cosmology into theory of nature and theory of mind betrays a relic of the Cartesian dualism and shows that biology was not yet a third division of science with principles of its own.

Before the rise of nineteenth-century biology, the process of generation in living organisms was conceived as a reproductive process, that is, a process by which the specific form of the parent organism was reproduced in the offspring. Any failure to reproduce it exactly was regarded as an aberration, a failure in the strict sense, a shot in which nature simply missed her mark. And of course there was a vast amount of evidence in favour of such a view; within our experience organic species remain relatively stable, and conspicuous aberrations from their form are in general either incapable of living or at least incapable of reproducing themselves. But palaeontology, as studied by the geologists of the eighteenth century, made it clear that over a longer stretch of time this evidence no longer held good; for geology very soon presented us with pictures of past ages in which the flora and fauna of the world had been very different from what they are now. The natural way of interpreting this new knowledge was by assuming that the organisms of to-day trace their pedigree not through a line of ancestors all specifically identical with themselves, but through these specifically different forms; so that the specific form itself undergoes change in time as the history of the world proceeds. This hypothesis was greatly strengthened, if not actually suggested, by the study of human history, where the forms of political and social organization can be seen to have undergone an evolution of the same kind. It was verified by the study, due especially to Darwin, of the breeding of domestic animals, where within comparatively short spaces of time human agency, by selecting certain strains to breed from, can produce forms having at any rate a strong resemblance to independent species and capable like them of breeding true to type.

These considerations led to an entirely new conception of the generative process. Whereas nature had hitherto been credited with an effort to reproduce fixed specific forms of life, she was henceforth conceived as attempting, like a human cattle-breeder, to produce always new and improved forms. But for the cattle-breeder an improved form means one better suited to the breeder's interests, which are not identical with the interests of the cattle themselves: thus the purposes of the breeder are imposed on the cattle from without. If nature is improving the forms of life, she works from within; and hence when we say that nature produces an improved form of life, what we mean is a form that is better fitted to survive or simply to live, i.e. a form more adequately embodying the idea of life. The history of life was thus conceived as the history of an endless succession of experiments on the part of nature to produce organisms more and more intensely and effectively alive. This conception of life was with great difficulty and severe struggles distinguished from the already familiar conceptions of matter and mind. The new biology thought of life as resembling matter and unlike mind in being wholly devoid of conscious purpose; Darwin talked freely of selection, and constantly used language implying teleology in organic nature, but he never for a moment thought of nature as a conscious agent deliberately trying experiments and aware of the ends which she was pursuing; if he had troubled to think out the philosophy underlying his biology he would have arrived at something like Schopenhauer's conception of the evolutionary process as the self-expression of a blind will, a creative and directive force utterly devoid of consciousness and of the moral attributes which consciousness bestows on the will of man; and it is some such ideas which we find floating everywhere in the atmosphere of Darwin's contemporaries, such as Tennyson. On the other hand, life was conceived as like mind and unlike matter in developing itself through an historic process, and orientating itself through this process not at random but in a determinate direction, towards the production of organisms more fitted to survive in the given environment, whatever that might be. If the environment changed, if, for example, a sea containing fishes very slowly dried up, the theory was that the fishes, generation by generation, would find means of adapting themselves to live first in mud and then on dry land; if it remained stable, the theory was that stronger and more active fishes would by degrees come into existence and crowd out or devour their less capable neighbours. This theory implied the philosophical conception of a life-force at once immanent and transcendent in relation to each and every living organism; immanent as existing only as embodied in these organisms, transcendent as seeking to realize itself not merely in the survival of the individual organisms, nor merely in the perpetuation of their specific type, but as always able and always trying to find for itself a more adequate realization in a new type.

This new philosophical conception of life as something different from both matter and mind was not established without opposition. This came, as was natural, from the heritage of the Cartesian two-substance theory, with its traditional inclusion of life within the realm of matter, and its consequent impulse to explain biological facts through the concepts of physics. The stronghold of this opposition was the theory that modifications in specific form depended on pure chance, paternal and maternal cells being shuffled and arranged in the fertilized ovum at random, and thus forming offspring of various kinds where some, owing to this inborn structure, were able to live in their environment and others were not. On the basis of this theory there has arisen an imposing structure of materialistic genetics, where by the word 'materialistic' I mean that it attempts to explain physiological function wholly in terms of physico-chemical structure. I cannot here go into the controversies, which are still lively, between views of this type and those of other schools, because these controversies really belong to the field of biology, and it is only their remoter implications that affect the philosophical questions I am here discussing. On the ground of philosophy, I think it is fair to say that the conception of vital process as distinct from mechanical or chemical change has come to stay, and has revolutionized our conception of nature. That many eminent biologists have not yet accepted it need cause no surprise. In the same way, the anti-Aristotelian physics which I have described as the new and fertile element in sixteenth-century cosmology was rejected by many distinguished scientists of that age; not only by futile pedants, but by men who were making important contributions to the advancement of knowledge.

§ 2. *Bergson*

This phase of thought, in which the idea of evolution was worked out as an essentially biological idea, may be conveniently regarded as culminating in the work of Bergson. I do not mean here to review that work as a whole, but only to indicate the main lines of what may be called the biological element in his philosophy and its relation to certain other elements.

Bergson's thought about life begins by firmly grasping the difference which marks it off from matter as understood by the physicist. There, everything that happens is the mere result of a cause already existing; matter and energy are constants, and all movements are predetermined and theoretically calculable; that is to say, there can never be anything really new; all future events are implied in any past event, or in Bergson's own phrase, *tout est donné*, the gates of the future are shut. In life, on the contrary, the gates of the future are open; the process of change is a creative process, leading to the appearance of genuine novelties. Here is a prima facie dualism within nature between a realm of matter and a realm of life. What are we to do with the dualism? Bergson approaches it through the theory of knowledge. There, too, he finds a dualism between intellect, which reasons and demonstrates, and works with rigid concepts, and is the appropriate organ for conceiving matter, and intuition, which enters into the life of its object, follows it in its movement, and is consequently the appropriate organ for cognizing the fluid and self-creative world of life. This second dualism Bergson attempts to resolve by maintaining that the human mind as a whole being a product of natural evolution, we need not suppose nature to have given us mental faculties in order to know the truth; in fact, our intellect is not a truth-knowing faculty at all, it is essentially a practical faculty, a faculty for enabling us to act effectively in the flux of nature by cutting this flux up into rigid chunks and thus manipulating it, much as a butcher manipulates animal flesh or a joiner manipulates trees. Thus Bergson has fallen back on a third dualism, a dualism between knowledge and action: knowledge conceived as essentially intuitive, the work of living consciousness steeping itself in its living object, and action conceived as manipulative, the work of that same consciousness detaching itself from its object and standing over against it in order to kill it, cut it up, and make things out of it.

These three dualisms turn into one another kaleidoscopically in Bergson's philosophy; but of the three the one which is fundamental for our purpose is the cosmological dualism between matter and life. We have already seen that life is the power or process which has created, among other things, the human mind, and that matter is a way in which this mind conceives reality for the purpose of manipulating it; but this reality, whatever else it is, is life itself; and since life and matter are opposites in every way it cannot therefore be matter too: consequently matter is a figment of the intellect, useful and necessary for purposes of action, but not true in any sense whatever. Thus matter is eliminated from Bergson's cosmology, and we are left with a world consisting simply and solely of the vital process and its products.

This process is described as a process of creative evolution. Efficient causes are banished from it as belonging merely to the fictitious world of matter; what moves in obedience to an efficient cause is merely pushed or pulled into motion, but life moves of itself, in obedience to its own inherent *élan vital*. But final causes are banished too; for in final causation the end is a ready-made datum, and therefore the process leading to that end must run on predetermined lines, and once more *tout est donné* and the absolute creativity or spontaneity of the process is denied. Bergson puts this by saying that teleology is only mechanism turned upside down—*un mécanisme au rebours*. The process of the world is a vast extemporization; the vital force has no aim, no goal, no guiding lights outside it or guiding principles within; it is sheer force, whose only inherent property is to flow, to push indefinitely onwards in any and every direction. Material things are not the vehicles or presuppositions of this cosmic movement, they are its products; and laws of nature are not the laws guiding its course, they are merely the shapes which for a time it adopts. Thus the old distinction between a substantial, extended, perceptible world of natural objects and the immaterial and unchanging intelligible laws which govern the behaviour of these objects—the Greek distinction between the perceptible and intelligible worlds—is denied in a new way, by resolving both terms alike into the concept of process or evolution, which produces at once the things which change and the changing laws of their changes.

The high and permanent merit of Bergson's theory of nature is that he is in earnest with the conception of life; he has grasped that conception with great firmness and defined it in a way which is not only brilliant and impressive but within its own limits conclusive. But when we look at his philosophy as a whole and see how he has attempted to identify this concept of life with the concept of nature, reducing everything in nature to the one term 'life', we see that he has done over again for life what the materialists of the seventeenth and eighteenth centuries did for matter. They took physics as their starting-point, and argued that, whatever else nature might be, it was at any rate material in the sense in which that word was understood by the physicists.

They then proceeded to reduce the entire world of nature to terms of matter. Bergson takes biology as his starting-point, and ends by reducing the whole world of nature to terms of life. We must ask whether this reduction is any more successful than the parallel reduction attempted by materialism.

Two questions arise here. First, are there any things which obstinately resist absorption into the concept of life, as mind resisted absorption into the concept of matter? And secondly, is the concept of life able to stand by itself as a cosmic principle, capable of doing its work when all other concepts have been knocked away from around it like a scaffolding?

The first question is one which the Bergsonian vitalism can face more confidently than the old materialism. The idea of life, bridging as it does the gap between matter and mind, can plausibly claim to explain both. I shall therefore not linger over that question.

The second is more serious. Life, as we know it, plays its part on a stage already set by matter. It is, so far as we can see, a local and transitory efflorescence on the surface of one among immense numbers of inorganic bodies. The inorganic world of astronomy and physics is a vast system with a range in space and time incalculably greater than that of the organic world. The fact that life ever and anywhere appears in this inorganic world is no doubt a fact throwing important light on the nature of the inorganic world; but when we extricate our minds from the spell of Bergson's eloquence and ask ourselves in a cool hour whether matter is a by-product of life, as he argues, or life a by-product of matter, as the materialists believe, we can hardly refuse to admit that the position he is defending is a monstrous and intolerable paradox. If we cannot seriously accept Kant's theory that nature is a by-product of the thinking activity of the human mind, because we are sure that the opposite is nearer the truth, how can we accept Bergson's very similar theory that the world of physics is a by-product of the self-creative activity of life? This is a new form of subjective idealism, of which we must say what Hume said of Berkeley's, that the argument might admit of no answer, but it produced no conviction.

This sense of the disproportions and paradoxes involved in Bergson's vitalism must lead us to a closer inspection of his fundamental concept. The life-force whose working creates both natural organisms and natural laws, and endows organisms with minds working intuitively for knowledge and intellectually for action, is a force outside of which and prior to which there is nothing; yet it differentiates itself, organizes itself in different ways, ramifies and develops on different lines, succeeds in developing along this line and fails to develop on that; here it congeals into stagnation, there it flows on with uninterrupted vigour. In short, throughout his detailed descriptions of its activity he thinks of it as if it were a river flowing among rocks and mountains which though they do not determine its movement do determine the ramifications and diversifications of that movement. This implies one of two things: either that the cause of these obstructions and ramifications is inherent in the life-force itself, or that this cause is something other than life. The first alternative is ruled out by Bergson's conception of life as pure activity, sheer infinite positive *élan*. We are therefore thrown back on the second, and compelled to think of this cause as something real in its own right, an obstruction to the flow of life; in short, a material world in which life develops and by whose agency the workings of life are conditioned; in a word, we come back to the idea of matter as the stage on which life plays its part. This is the vicious circle of Bergson's cosmology: ostensibly he regards matter as a by-product of life, but actually he cannot explain how that or any other special by-product can arise without presupposing, alongside of and indeed prior to life, matter itself.

This conclusion is fatal to Bergson's theory of knowledge. If matter is no less real than life, the intellect which thinks the material world is no less an organ of knowledge than the intuition which envisages life, his sceptical or pragmatist attitude towards physics and in general logical thinking breaks down, and we are forced to admit that the intellect in dissecting the world and solidifying the fragments of it into conceptual units is not falsifying reality for practical ends, but dividing reality (as Plato put it) at its joints, discerning divisions in it that really exist. Consequently Bergson's theory of intuition must go too; it is no longer possible to restrict knowledge to a mere immediate consciousness which life has of itself, a consciousness as fluid and changeful as that of which it is conscious; and we come back to the idea of consciousness as rising to the level of knowledge only when it is ballasted with logic, somewhat as Bergson speaks of space as ballasted with geometry. Just as the stream of life presupposes the topography of a material world through which it flows, so the stream of consciousness presupposes the topography of logical and conceptual forms, categories, or ideas in the Platonic and Hegelian sense; and Bergson's attempt to deny these two presuppositions leaves him in the dilemma of either tacitly asserting what he professes to deny or else asserting nothing except the existence of a force which does nothing and of an intuition which apprehends that nothingness.

What is wrong with Bergson's philosophy, regarded as a cosmology, is not the fact that he takes life seriously but the fact that he takes nothing else seriously. The concept of life is a most important clue to the general nature of the world, but it is not, as Bergson has tried to make it, an adequate definition of the world as a whole. The inanimate world of the physicist is a dead weight on Bergson's metaphysics; he can do nothing with it except try to digest it in the stomach of his life-process; but it proves indigestible. Yet the advance in the theory of nature which Bergson has achieved by fixing his attention on life cannot be denied. We cannot ignore Bergson's work; what we must do is to reconsider the concept which he has found intractable, the concept of dead matter.

II

MODERN PHYSICS

THIS leads us to physics, as the science in whose hand the cards should lie for the next stage in the game, very much as, a century earlier, the cards lay in the hand of biology. We all know that the leading conceptions of physics have been profoundly modified in the last fifty years, and it is these modifications which I must now try to describe; but this is far harder to do than it is to give an account of the rise of evolutionary biology, because the change is so recent that our ideas have not yet been readjusted to it, and its effects, instead of having been long digested in popular handbooks, are at present chiefly embodied in technical works that are unintelligible to a layman like myself. Consequently everything I can say on this subject is very tentative, and in saying anything at all I am acutely conscious that I may be making the most serious mistakes. But I cannot shirk the responsibility of saying something, because, so far as I can understand these new ideas, they seem to carry implications of the greatest importance for the philosophical view of nature and its relation to mind.

§ 1. *The old theory of matter*

First, then, I must try to describe how the world of nature was conceived before these changes began. It was conceived as divided into solid particles moving in space. Each particle, physically considered, was atomic: that is to say, physically indivisible and indestructible; but it was not geometrically indivisible, that is, it had a certain size and shape. But it could not be defined without residue in geometrical terms, for it had certain physical, as distinct from geometrical, properties, of which the most fundamental was impenetrability. In virtue of its impenetrability it could never occupy the same place as any other particle: that is, at any given moment it had a place of its own, in which it was entirely situated and in which no other particle was contained. Since any particle might move in any direction, it was always possible for the paths of two particles to intersect so as to bring both to the same place at the same time; then they collided, and the impact would change the direction of their movements. Further, each particle possessed inertia, in virtue of which it would move with uniform velocity in a straight line, if in motion, or remain for ever stationary, if at rest; and such uniform motion or rest would persist until interfered with by the impact of another particle. This was the corpuscular or atomic theory of matter inherited by the seventeenth century from the Greek atomists and accepted by scientists of the next two centuries as expressing the fundamental truth about the physical world.

So far the conception seems comprehensible enough, though there are serious difficulties, when one examines it more closely, arising out of such questions as these: What is the exact relation of a body to the space which it is said to occupy? How can motion be transferred by impact from one body to another? Why should bodies move, instead of being all at rest? and so on. But, neglecting these difficulties, it gives us a clearly imaginable picture, even if not a clearly intelligible theory, of the material world.

§ 2. *Its complications and inconsistencies*

As early as Newton, however, this simple conception was complicated by the addition of a new element. Newton maintained that every particle of matter acted as if it possessed an attractive force acting upon every other particle with a strength directly proportional to the product of their masses and inversely to the square of the distance between them. Now this gravitational force appears as a second cause of motion, conceived as existing side by side with impact: some movements appear to be due to the one, some to the other. Such a doctrine, in the crude dualistic form in which I have stated it, is tolerable neither in philosophy nor in science; for each alike is committed to searching for principles unifying the things which they study, and a serious physicist would never suggest that some movements are due to impact and others to the totally different agency of attraction without asking himself how these two principles are related to each other. Newton himself felt the difficulty so strongly that he more than once explicitly denied the doctrine of an inherent gravitational force belonging to matter as such. These are his words in writing to Bentley (25 Feb. 169$\frac{2}{3}$):

'That gravity should be innate, inherent and essential to matter, so that one body may act upon another at a distance, through a vacuum, without the mediation of anything else through which their action may be conveyed from one to another, is to me so great an absurdity that I believe no man who has in philosophical matters a competent faculty of thinking, can ever fall into it.'

He believed that gravity must be either a peculiar effect of some peculiar kind of impact, which he always regarded as the only possible physical cause of motion, or the effect of some immaterial cause. And right down into the middle of the nineteenth century distinguished physicists over and over again repeated Newton's objections, and no one ever answered them. It remained a standing reproach to what is nowadays called the classical physics, that it never even approached a satisfactory solution of the question, What is the relation between these two apparently disparate causes of motion, impact and gravitation ?

Complications did not end here. Newton had conceived the space in which his particles moved as a vacuum; but later physicists found themselves obliged to think of it as filled with something called ether, which was required in order to explain the behaviour of light. The ether was another kind of matter altogether; it was not divided into particles, it was uniform and homogeneous, and its function was to propagate wave-like disturbances caused by the movements of the particles. It was therefore stationary, all movements being movements through it; but it offered no resistance to these movements, although it pervaded all space and was at once elastic and perfectly rigid.

The difficulty of reconciling these two conceptions, the so-called gross matter and the ether, was always obvious to physicists, and attempts of every kind were made to overcome the difficulty. On the one hand, the attempt was made over and over again to ascribe a corpuscular structure to the ether, that is, to conceive it as a highly rarefied gas, or again to conceive light as a stream of moving particles, which would make it possible to do without ether altogether; but both attempts broke down in the face of experimental facts. On the other hand, an attempt was made to think of gross matter as composed of local disturbances or nucleations in the ether, but this contradicted the fundamental notion of the ether as essentially homogeneous and stationary.

A third complication arose from the side of chemistry. John Dalton succeeded in identifying a number of kinds of matter each having its own qualitatively peculiar ways of behaving; these elements, as they were called, were regarded as consisting of kinds of atoms each having its own physical peculiarities. But the atoms, as particles of gross matter, could have no properties except quantitative ones; it was therefore assumed, and the assumption was verified by experiment, that the atoms of one element differed in mass or weight from those of another. Hence the ultimate particles of matter had to be regarded not as uniform in their quantity of mass but as varying according to a scale, the scale of atomic weights. Now, quite apart from the impossibility of bridging the gulf between physical quantity and chemical quality—that is, of showing why a body with one atomic weight should behave in a specific chemical manner when one with a slightly different atomic weight behaved in quite another—the corpuscular theory of matter, from the physicist's point of view, required the assumption that all atoms had the same mass, for that theory regarded the atom or primordial particle of matter essentially as a unit of mass. For this reason, just as there was fifty years ago one open conflict between the theory of gross matter and that of ether, so there was another between the view of gross matter required by physics and that required by chemistry.

I refer to these old problems and controversies, which figure so largely in the scientific literature of two generations ago, because the situation produced by modern discoveries and theories in physics is so strange that people are often tempted to sigh for the good old days of what they call classical physics, when people believed in a simple and comprehensible theory of matter as composed of particles moving about in absolute space; and it is worth while to remember that this supposedly simple theory existed only in the popular handbooks, which offered to the general public a façade of imposing consistency behind which were concealed the liveliest dissensions and the most painful doubts concerning the very doctrines that were assumed in the handbooks as fundamental and unquestioned.

§ 3. *The new theory of matter*

Modern physics, whatever the difficulties to which it has led, has at least done something towards removing these scandals. Taking the last of them first, the quarrel between chemistry and physics has been settled by the electron theory, according to which the chemical atom is not an ultimate corpuscle but a constellation of electrons, so that atoms with one set of chemical qualities can be changed into atoms with another set by knocking an electron off them. Thus we get back to a single physical unit, the electron; but we also get a very important new conception of chemical quality, as depending not upon the merely quantitative aspect of the atom, its weight, but upon the pattern formed by the electrons that compose it. This pattern is not a static pattern but a dynamic pattern, a pattern constantly changing in a definite rhythmical way, like the rhythmical patterns discovered by the Pythagoreans in the field of acoustics.

This idea of rhythmical pattern as a link between quantity and quality is important in the modern theory of nature not only as providing a connexion between those hitherto unconnected notions, but, what is more important still, as revealing a new significance in the idea of time. If an atom of hydrogen possesses the qualities of hydrogen not merely because it consists of a certain number of electrons, nor even merely because those atoms are arranged in a certain way, but because they move in a certain rhythmical way, it follows that within a given instant of time the atom does not possess those qualities at all; it only possesses them in a tract of time long enough for the rhythm of the movement to establish itself. It had of course always been known that there were certain things which could only exist in a tract of time and could not exist at a single instant. Motion is the most obvious case: *at* an instant there is no difference between a body in motion and a body at rest. Life, too, is a fairly obvious case: the only thing that differentiates a living body from one just dead is that in the living animal certain rhythmical processes and changes are going on which are absent from the dead body. Hence life, like motion, is a thing that takes time and has no instantaneous existence. Aristotle showed that the same is true of moral qualities: happiness, for example, according to him, is a thing which belongs to a man at all only if it belongs to him throughout a lifetime (ἐν βίῳ τελείῳ), so that an instantaneous view of his mental state could not distinguish whether he was happy or not, just as an instantaneous photograph could not distinguish a living animal from a dead, or a body in motion from a body at rest (cf.

pp. 19–22 above). But before the arrival of modern physics it had always been supposed that movement is merely an accident that happens to a body, and that the body enjoys its own proper nature irrespective of such accidents; a body is what it is, people thought, at every instant of its history, and nothing that can happen to it can alter its physical attributes. This new theory of the atom as a moving pattern of electrons changed all that, and assimilated the chemical properties of matter to the moral qualities of a mind or the vital qualities of an organism in making them a function of time. Henceforth, just as in ethics you admittedly cannot separate what a man is from what he does, nor in biology what an organism is from what it does, so in physics you cannot separate what matter is from what it does. That separation was the foundation-stone of the so-called classical physics, which conceived motion as something external, added to a matter which already enjoyed its own proper attributes independently of such addition, and believed that an instantaneous photograph of the material world would reveal its entire nature.

Here, in the electronic theory of valency, we see the old theory of matter, which Bergson is still assuming to be true, dissolving away and giving place to a new theory in which matter is essentially process or activity or something very much like life. But this new theory makes no concessions to animism or hylozoism or any confusion between the vital process in an organism and the physical process in an atom. The difference between these two kinds of process is not forgotten when this very important resemblance is discovered. Hence, when under the stimulus of these new theories of matter a philosopher like Whitehead declares that the whole of reality is an organism, or one like Alexander describes time as the mind of which space is the body, it would be misunderstanding them to accuse them of reverting to the old Greek view of nature as a living thing; they are not merging physics in biology as Bergson might have liked to do, they are welcoming a new view of physics which for the first time in modern history reveals a fundamental similarity, instead of an indefinite series of contrasts, between the world of matter and the world of life.

Let us now consider the dualism between impact and attraction, and ask how recent physics deals with that. When we remember that for Newton the only hope seemed to be the denial of real attractive forces and their reduction to terms of impact, the novelty of recent physics is strikingly shown by the fact that it takes the opposite line, denies impact as a *vera causa* altogether, and reduces it to a special case of attraction and repulsion. According to the new theory of matter, no particle of matter ever comes into contact with another particle. Every particle is surrounded by a field of force, conceived on the analogy of the magnetic field; and when one body bounces off another this is not because of an impact of body upon body, it is because of a repulsion analogous to that by which the north poles of two magnetic needles repel one another.

Here again the fundamental concept of matter reveals a profound alteration in its structure. The old idea was that first of all a given piece of matter is what it is, and then, because it enjoys that permanent and unchanging nature, it acts on various occasions in various ways. It is because a body, in itself or inherently, possesses a certain mass, that it exerts a certain force in impact or in attracting others. But now the energies belonging to material bodies not only explain their action upon each other, they explain the extension and the mass of each body by itself; for a cubic inch of iron only occupies a cubic inch because of the equilibrium between the attractive and repulsive forces of the atoms composing it, and these again are only atoms of iron because of the rhythmical patterns set up by the attractive and repulsive forces of their constituent electrons. Hence not only chemical qualities but even physical and quantitative properties are now conceived as a function of activity. So far from its being true that matter does what it does because first of all, independently of what it does, it is what it is, we are now taught that matter is what it is because it does what it does: or, to be more precise, its being what it is is the same thing as its doing what it does. Once more, then, and now not only in chemistry but in the more fundamental field of physics, a new similarity has emerged between matter on the one hand and mind and life on the other: matter is no longer contrasted with mind and life as a realm in which being is independent of acting and logically prior to it, it resembles them as a third realm in which being is at bottom simply acting.

In order to show that these implications are clearly recognized by scientifically trained philosophers of to-day, let me quote a short passage from Whitehead, whose earlier career as a mathematician and physicist is being so brilliantly continued by his work as a philosopher:

'The older point of view enables us to abstract from change and to conceive of the full reality of Nature *at an instant*, in abstraction from any temporal duration and characterized as to its interrelations solely by the instantaneous distribution of matter in space. According to the Newtonian view, what had been thus omitted was the change of distribution at neighbouring instants. But such change was, on this view, plainly irrelevant to the essential reality of the material universe at the instant considered. Locomotion . . . was accidental and not essential. Equally essential was endurance. . . . For the modern view process, activity, and change are the matter of fact. At an instant there is nothing. Each instant is only a way of grouping matters of fact. Thus, since there are no instants, conceived as simple primary entities, there is no Nature at an instant.' (*Nature and Life*, 1934, pp. 47–8.)

After this it is hardly necessary to reconsider the dualism between gross matter and ether; for gross matter, consisting of bodies identical at each instant of time and possessed of intrinsic extension and mass, has disappeared. The ether, too, has disappeared, owing to the Michelson-Morley experiment, which proved conclusively that light is not a disturbance propagated through a stationary medium. But a very curious relic of the old dualism still survives in the physics of to-day. It has been proved by modern physicists that not only light-rays, but all electrons, behave in a curiously ambiguous manner. Sometimes they behave like particles, sometimes like waves. The question is then asked, Which are they really? They can hardly be both; for if an electron were a particle it could not behave like a wave, and if it were a wave it could not sometimes behave like a particle. Hence one physicist has described his own state of mind by saying that he believes in the corpuscular theory on Mondays, Wednesdays, and Fridays, and in the undulatory theory on Tuesdays, Thursdays, and Saturdays. Now it seems clear that the corpuscular theory is simply the ghost of the idea of gross matter in the classical physics, and the undulatory theory the ghost of the idea of ether. When ideas are dead their ghosts usually walk; but no ghost walks for ever, and the main thing is for the people they haunt to remember that they are only ghosts. On the modern theory of matter the electron cannot be a particle, for a particle means a particle of gross matter being what it is independently of doing what it does. Nor can it be a wave, for a wave means a disturbance in an elastic medium which possesses its properties of extension and elasticity independently of being thus disturbed.

If electrons and protons merely sometimes behaved like particles and sometimes like waves, the situation would be serious. But there is a law governing these differences of behaviour. I quote from Sir James Jeans (*The New Background of Science*, 1933, p. 163): electrons and protons behave 'as particles while they travel freely through space, and as waves when they encounter matter'. And further, 'there is a complete mathematical theory which shows how in all such cases the particle- and wave-pictures are merely two aspects of the same reality, so that light can appear sometimes as particles and sometimes as waves, but never as both at the same time. It also explains how the same can be true of electrons and protons'. The mathematics of the theory to which Jeans refers—Heisenberg's theory of wave-mechanics—are entirely beyond me, but I am only concerned with its metaphysics. And from this point of view the theory is very far from being absurd.

Suppose we take seriously the modern view that not only mind and life but matter too is inherently and essentially activity. Suppose, too, that the activity which constitutes and is the material world is an activity distributed over space and developing through time. It will then follow that what we call a particle of matter is a focus of activity, spatially related to other such foci. Its activity will necessarily have a double character: first in relation to itself, and secondly in its relation to other so-called particles. In its relation to itself it is a self-developing and thus self-maintaining process: something self-contained and enduring, something to which the old metaphysical term of substance can be applied. In this self-maintaining activity we may well compare the electron of modern physics with the Leibnitian monad. In its relation to any other electron it is an activity impinging upon that other from without; it is now simply a disturbance in the environment, a field of force in which the other finds itself as an iron filing may find itself within the field of a magnet. If we remember that the electron simply is what it does, that its substance is nothing but its activity, we shall find no difficulty in seeing that the real or substantial being of the electron must have this double character: we shall no longer say that it *is* one thing but in certain circumstances behaves as if it were another, still less that it *is* some third mysterious thing which now behaves in this way and now in that; we shall say that the same activity which in its relation to itself presents one character necessarily presents the other character in its relation to others like itself. Anyone who tries to express this idea in terms of the old dualism between gross matter and ether will say, exactly as Jeans does say, that free-moving electrons resemble particles of gross matter, but an electron encountering another will resemble a disturbance in the ether by which this other is surrounded. And anyone who realizes that gross matter and ether are not ideas but only ghosts of ideas will be quite undismayed by this appearance of contradiction, and will emphasize it in order to show that he knows how dead those ideas really are.

Thus the modern theory of matter has solved all the three dualisms on which I have laid stress: the dualism of impact and attraction, the dualism of ether and gross matter, and the dualism of physical quantity and chemical quality. But I mentioned certain other problems which perplexed the Newtonian form of modern physics: the dualism of matter and motion, the problem of the transference of motion from body to body, and the dualism of matter and space. It is incumbent upon modern physics to solve these too, and we must ask whether the new conception of matter can do it.

The dualism of matter and motion disappears. That dualism depends on thinking of motion as an accident of matter, and of matter as something having all its own inherent characteristics complete at any given moment, whether it moves or not. From this it followed that there is no inherent reason in matter why it should ever move, or why it should be at rest either; having its own nature completely realized at any given moment, it has no reason for existing at all at any other moment; which is why Descartes said that God must create the world afresh at every instant of time. But modern physical theory regards matter as possessing its own characteristics, whether chemical or physical, only because it moves; time is therefore a factor in its very being, and that being is fundamentally motion.

The transference of motion from body to body also disappears. All bodies are in motion all the time, and since this motion is activity it must display itself in the double form of immanent activity and transeunt activity, so that every body must act both on itself, as moving itself, and also act on others as moving them.

§ 4. *The finitude of nature*

There remains the dualism of matter and space: or rather, since time is now a factor in the being of matter, the dualism between matter and space-time. Matter is an activity which goes on in space and takes time; what is the relation between the space and time which this activity occupies and the activity which occupies it?

Unlike Newton, the modern physicist recognizes no empty space. Matter is activity, and therefore a body is where it acts; and because every particle of matter acts all over the universe, every body is everywhere. This doctrine again is explicitly taught by Whitehead. It may seem a flat denial of the extension or spread-out-ness of matter, which implies that every piece of matter is outside every other; but it is not really that, for these various overlapping and interpenetrating activities have each its own focus or centre, and in its self-maintaining aspect the body in question is situated at that centre and nowhere else. Consequently the modern doctrine, though it denies Newton's theory of empty space, does not assert the opposite or Cartesian doctrine that all space is full of matter; for matter, in that doctrine, meant not activity or energy but gross matter.

All physicists are now committed to the theory of relativity. In its narrower and earlier form this theory consisted in the doctrine that the physical and chemical activities of any two bodies, A and B, though they are both affected by a change of distance between the two, are not in any way differently affected according as A is at rest and B in motion, or B at rest and A in motion. In its wider form, as stated by Einstein in 1916, it extends this doctrine to cover motions of every kind, for example, when A is at rest and B revolves round it, or B is at rest and A rotates on its own axis. It comes to this, that

physics now finds that it has no need for the conceptions of
absolute rest or absolute motion: all it needs is the conceptions
of relative rest and relative motion. And this implies that
physics has no use for the conception of absolute situation or
absolute size; all it needs is the conception of one thing's
situation or size relatively to another.[1]

This is all very well for the physicist, but its cosmological
implications are alarming. Classical physics in the time of
Newton, as I have already explained, began with a cosmological picture taken over from the Greek atomists; and according to them space must extend, uniform and infinite, in every
direction, whether or not there is anything in it, and time must
be infinite in the same sense. Now, if space is all full of fields
of force, it will follow that at every point in space there are
infinite forces impinging from every side upon any piece of
matter situated there; and consequently, since these forces will
cancel out, none of them will act on that piece of matter at all.
Determinate events happen at this or that point in space only
because determinate forces are at work there; and determinate
means finite. Consequently, as Einstein pointed out, we must
think of the material world, and therefore of space, as finite;
and we must answer Lucretius' question, What would happen
if you went to the edge of space and threw a spear outwards, by
saying that within this finite universe all possible paths along
which matter or radiation can travel are curved paths, so that
they are infinite in the sense of returning infinitely upon themselves, though finite in the sense of being confined within a

---

[1] [One has to distinguish, in the theory of relativity, between the objects of
the theory and the procedure by which those objects are attained. Einstein's
general relativity of 1916 is not merely, or solely, an extension of the *doctrine*
stated by Collingwood to other kinds of relative motion; its feature is that it
provides rules of procedure by which the consequences of a certain set of views
about nature may be obtained. It devises a procedure by which any one
observer A, from his own description of a phenomenon, can infer the description of the same phenomenon that would be made by any second observer B
whatever, provided B's position and motion relative to A have been determined
by A; the passage from observer A to observer B is called, in technical language,
'changing the co-ordinates'. The rules of procedure are transitive and sym-
metrical: we can start with A or with B, without attempting to attach a
meaning to saying either that A is at rest, and B in motion, or that B is at
rest, and A is in motion—although with one of the observers the phenomenon
in question will have different spatio-temporal relations from what it has with
the other.—E. A. M.]

determinate volume which is the volume of the universe. Corresponding to this spatial finitude of the universe, there has arisen the idea of its temporal finitude. The spectra of the spiral nebulae have revealed facts which appear to show that they are travelling outwards from a common centre, and this has resulted in the theory that the physical universe originated at a date not infinitely remote in the past, in something resembling an explosion of energy which at once began time and began, in time, to generate space.

It is easy to insist that this event, since it admittedly had a date, must have implied time before it, just as it is easy to insist that an expanding universe, or even a finite universe not expanding, implies space around it. But it is not so easy to answer the question, What, if anything, is meant by such insistence? whether, that is to say, we really have any idea of a time in which nothing happens and a space in which nothing is situated, and if so what these ideas are. On the one hand, the ideas of space and time seem to be nothing but abstractions from the idea of movement; on the other, they seem to be logical presuppositions of that idea. Modern physics finds it possible to treat them as abstractions from it; but philosophical thought from the time of Kant onward has been accustomed to treat them as presuppositions.

Suppose, however, that philosophical thought is right here. If space and time are logically prior to movement, not mere abstractions from it, does it follow that, cosmologically speaking, that is, speaking not of logical presuppositions but of real existence, space and time need actually exist before movements begin and outside the region where movements are going on? To argue in that way is to hypostatize concepts, to attribute actual existence to something which in reality has only logical being. Precisely as Thales thought of matter as something which must have actually existed before the world was made of it, whereas matter in the Greek sense of the term is only a logical abstraction, so the critics of modern science who boggle at the idea of a finite universe are thinking of empty space and time as two kinds of emptiness which must actually exist before and outside that universe, whereas they are really only its logical presuppositions, not the actual matrix in which it lies like a crystal or the empty womb in which it was formed like a child.

Greek thought, developing and criticizing Thales' conception of matter, came to the conclusion that matter really meant potentiality, so that to speak of matter as existing before the world would only mean that before the world came into existence there was the possibility of its doing so. In the same spirit, it might perhaps be argued that empty space-time, which is the ghost of the old idea of matter, really means the potentiality of movement; so that if we insist upon the idea of a time before the physical world began, and of a space outside its limits, we are only insisting that there must be something prior to it and transcending it, in which the possibility of its origin and existence is grounded. But this priority is a logical priority, not a temporal priority; and this transcendence is a logical transcendence, not spatial outwardness.

This at any rate seems clear: that since modern science is now committed to a view of the physical universe as finite, certainly in space and probably in time, the activity which this same science identifies with matter cannot be a self-created or ultimately self-dependent activity. The world of nature or physical world as a whole, on any such view, must ultimately depend for its existence on something other than itself. And here modern science agrees with Plato and Aristotle, with Galileo and Newton, with Kant and Hegel: in a word, modern science, after an experiment in materialism, has come back into line with the main tradition of European thought, which has always ascribed to nature an essentially derivative or dependent status in the general scheme of things. It is true that the most varied proofs have been offered as to why nature must be dependent, and the most varied theories as to what it depended on; but in general, with strikingly few exceptions, scientists and philosophers have agreed that the world of nature forms only one part or aspect of all being, and that in this total realm its place is a secondary one, one of dependence on something prior to itself. This traditional view was certainly denied by the Greek atomists; it was denied by John the Scot, who went so far as to identify nature not only with the sum total of what is but with the sum total of what is *plus* the sum total of what is not; and it was again denied by the materialism which formed a popular and influential strain in the European thought of the nineteenth century; but this materialism rested on the notion of matter which as I have shown was exploded by the scientific work of the last thirty or forty years, and it only lingers now in corners and lumber-rooms of thought where the new discoveries have not penetrated.

This is the reason why modern scientific leaders like Eddington and Jeans talk about God in a way that would have scandalized most scientists of fifty years ago. Having worked out their theory of matter to a point where the essential finitude and dependency of the physical world become clear, they give the traditional name of God to that upon which it depends. And the use of this traditional name is to be welcomed not only on account of the hope it brings of healing the nineteenth-century breach between science and religion, not only because it indicates a return to the main philosophical tradition of Plato, Aristotle, and Descartes, but also because it reveals the extent to which modern thought is disentangling itself from the cobwebs of subjective idealism. The justly revered authority of Kant would suggest a very different conclusion: namely, that if nature bears on its face the marks of depending for its existence on something else, that something is the human mind. Attempts have been made to capture relativity and other modern theories, with their obviously anti-materialistic tendency, in the interests of subjective idealism ; and there are scientists who aid and abet these attempts, and use subjective idealism as a kind of bomb-proof shelter in which to escape from criticism of their own conception of nature: for this, they say, is after all only a conception framed by the human mind with its notoriously limited faculties of comprehension, and it is only natural that such a conception should be found lacking in coherence. This is bad philosophy, for it implies that we both can and cannot transcend our own cognitive faculties: can transcend them, for otherwise we should be unable to recognize their limitations and the badness of the conclusions to which they lead us, and cannot transcend them, for otherwise we should be able to overcome the limitations and better the conclusions. The most vigorous thought of our own time, scientific and philosophical alike, has turned resolutely away from these subjectivist or pheno-menalist doctrines, and agrees that whatever nature depends on it does not depend on the human mind.

But although the doctrine expressed by scientists like Eddington and Jeans that nature or the material world depends on God is welcome as marking their rejection both of materialism and of subjectivism, these are merely negative merits. If the doctrine is to stand for anything positive, we must know not only that God is something other than either matter or the human mind, but what that other is. For Eddington, who stands closest to the religious tradition, the non-material reality on which material nature depends is mind: that is to say, he conceives God as mind. His argument on this point, however (it is stated in his Gifford Lectures on *The Nature of the Physical World*, 1928), seems to me to be tainted with relics of phenomenalism: he thinks of nature as in the last resort appearance, and of mind as that to which it appears. Jeans, converging rather with Plato, thinks of the immaterial reality on which nature depends for its existence primarily as a complex of mathematical forms, and secondly, quite in the Platonic manner, as a God who thinks these forms, a geometrician-God. But here, too, there seems to be a subjectivist element, though of a subtler type, in the dependence of the ideal objective mathematical order upon the mind of an absolute mathematician.

III

MODERN COSMOLOGY

FROM the somewhat slender metaphysical threads of argument in the writings of mathematical physicists we must turn to the work of the professed philosophers, and of these I shall deal only with two, Alexander and Whitehead. Each of these is a philosophical genius of very high order, and their works mark a return to the grand manner of philosophical writing, the manner which we last saw in English when Hume gave us his *Treatise of Human Nature.* This grand manner is not the mark of a period; it is the mark of a mind which has its philosophical material properly controlled and digested. It is thus based on width and steadiness of outlook upon the subject-matter; it is essentially objective, concerned not with the thoughts of others, whether to criticize or expound, but with the features of the thing itself; it is marked by calmness of temper and candour of statement, no difficulties being concealed and nothing set down in malice or passion. All great philosophers have this calmness of mind, all passion spent by the time their vision is clear, and they write as if they saw things from a mountain-top. That is the tone which distinguishes a great philosopher; a writer who lacks it may or may not be worth reading, but he certainly falls short of greatness.

§ 1. *Alexander*

We will begin, then, by considering how it is that the world of nature has appeared to Alexander from his mountain-top. This world, as it exists in its ceaseless changes, appears to him[1] as a single cosmic process in which there emerge, as it goes on, higher orders of being. The word 'emergent' is borrowed from Lloyd Morgan who used it in his *Instinct and Experience* (1912) and who later set forth in his *Emergent Evolution* (1923) a similar view of the world as an evolutionary process; he used the word 'emergent' to show that the higher orders of being are not mere resultants of what went before and were not contained in them as an effect is in its efficient cause: thus the higher is not a mere modification or complication of the lower but something

---

[1] *Space, Time, and Deity* (2 vols., 1920): Gifford Lectures, 1916–18.

genuinely and qualitatively new, which must be explained not by reducing it to terms of the lower out of which it grew but according to its own proper principles. Thus, according to Lloyd Morgan, life has emerged from matter and mind from life; but that does not imply that life is merely matter and that biology should be reduced to a special case of physics, nor that mind is merely life and that the sciences of mind are to be resolved into biology and so ultimately into physics. Lloyd Morgan's argument makes no claim to show why a new order of beings should emerge from an old, or why things should emerge in any determinate sequence; his method is, and professes to be, purely descriptive. And here I must refer to General Smuts's amplification of the same idea, in his book on *Holism and Evolution* (1926): more frankly philosophical in his outlook than Lloyd Morgan, he has attempted to state the principle of emergence by saying that nature is permeated by an impulse towards the creation of wholes, or self-contained individuals, and to show how each stage of evolution is marked by the emergence of a new and more adequate type of individuality embracing and transcending as parts of itself the individuals previously existing.

Alexander's view of evolution is closely akin to both these. He accepts the general scheme (a commonplace since Hegel) of life as emerging from matter and mind from life, and he holds that in both these emergences—and similarly in all others—the essence of the process is that, first, there exist things with a determinate structure and character of their own, and then, that these things arrange themselves into a new pattern which as a whole possesses a new type of structure and a new order of qualities. The fundamental conception here implied is the conception that quality depends on pattern. This, as I have already said, is the conception by which the Pythagoreans explained musical notes and by which modern science explains chemical quality. Alexander boldly extends it to evolution as a whole. He begins with space-time, not space and time as two separate entities in the Newtonian manner, but a single entity in which, to use his own expression, space is metaphorically the body, and time, as the principle of organization, the mind; without space there could be no time, and without time no space. Thus we get, not one infinite plurality of points and another of instants, located respectively in space and time, but a single infinite plurality of point-instants, which are the ultimate constituents of all that exists. Hence everything that exists has a place-aspect and also a time-aspect. In its place-aspect it has a determinate situation; in its time-aspect it is always moving to a new situation; and thus Alexander arrives metaphysically at the modern conception of matter as inherently possessed of motion, and of all movements as relative to each other within space-time as a whole. The first emergence is the emergence of matter itself from point-instants: a particle of matter is a moving pattern of point-instants, and because this is always a determinate pattern it will have a determinate quality. This is the metaphysical exposition of the modern theory of matter; and here, as often elsewhere in his argument, Alexander is careful to point out that quality is not a mere phenomenon, it does not exist merely because it appears to a mind; it exists as a function of structure in the objective world. This applies not only to chemical qualities but to the so-called secondary qualities of matter, colour, and the like, which are functions of patterns themselves composed of material elements: thus a particular musical note is the quality intrinsically belonging to a certain rhythm in air-vibrations, and is real irrespective of whether or not there are ears to hear it. Thus, in the physical world before the emergence of life, there are already various orders of being, each consisting of a pattern composed of elements belonging to the order next below it: point-instants form a pattern which is the electron having physical qualities, electrons form an atom having chemical qualities, atoms form a molecule having chemical qualities of a new and higher order, molecules like those of air form wave-patterns having sonority, and so on.

Living organisms in their turn are patterns whose elements are bits of matter. In themselves these bits of matter are inorganic; it is only the whole pattern which they compose that is alive, and its life is the time-aspect or rhythmic process of its material parts. Thus life is the time-aspect of the organism, its space-aspect being inorganic matter; in other words, life is a peculiar kind of activity or process belonging to a body composed of parts which taken in themselves enjoy an activity of the next lower order.

Mind is a further peculiar kind of activity arising in living organisms and using life as its substratum or material: thus mind is a pattern of vital activities. Just as life is qualitatively different from any activity belonging to the material of the organic body, so mind is qualitatively different from any activity belonging to life as such. Again, just as there are different orders of being within matter, so there are different orders of life, higher and lower, the higher being elaborated forms of the lower, and different orders of mind. 'Ascent takes place, it would seem, through complexity. But at each change of quality the complexity as it were gathers itself together and is expressed in a new simplicity. The emergent quality is the summing together into a new totality of the component materials' (ii. 70).

This evolutionary process is theoretically infinite. At present, it has reached the stage of mind; but it only goes forward at all because at every stage there is a forward movement or impulse, a nisus or drive, towards the realization of the next. Mind, among its other peculiarities, has the privilege of being conscious of this drive and conceiving in its thought the goal towards which its evolution is leading it. Hence every mind has a conception of a higher form of mentality into which it is consciously endeavouring to convert itself; these conceptions are the ideals which govern human conduct and thought. But mind as a whole, being only one stage in the cosmic process, is engaged in an endeavour to evolve out of itself something as different from itself as mind is different from life, something which when it appears will be on its material side a pattern of mental activities as mind is a pattern of vital activities, but on its formal or qualitative side something altogether new. This next higher order of quality, as yet unrealized, is deity, and thus God is the being towards whose emergence the evolutionary nisus of mind is directed.

I cannot here pause to indicate the innumerable ways in which this argument, so classically severe and simple in its architectural lines, is verified and defended in detail; still less to point out its many affinities with the cosmological theories of other great philosophers. I must go back to the beginning and raise the question, Upon what foundations or presuppositions does the cosmic process, as conceived by Alexander, rest? For

Plato, for Hegel, and for modern Platonists like Jeans, it rests on an eternal order of immaterial forms or categories. Alexander has a theory of his own concerning categories: he regards them not in the Platonic or Hegelian manner as transcending or presupposed by empirical things, but simply as immanent in them, wherever and whenever they exist: that is, he considers them as nothing else than the pervasive or omnipresent characteristics of whatever exists in space-time. Thus space-time, for him, generates with one hand, as it were, the categories, as hallmarks which it stamps upon all its creatures; and with the other the order of empirical existents, each possessing its own peculiar qualities but all alike marked with the categorial characteristics of identity, diversity, existence, universality, particularity, individuality, relation, order, causality, reciprocity, quantity, intensity, wholeness and partness, motion, unity and plurality. Space-time is the source of the categories, but they do not apply to space-time; they belong only to what exists, and what exists is not space-time itself but only the empirical things in it; but these things possess categorial characteristics for one reason and one only—namely, that they exist in space-time. Hence Alexander regards them as depending on the nature of space-time: that is, he aims at deducing them from the definition of space-time as its necessary consequences.

Now this doctrine of space-time as logically prior to the categories demands close attention. Superficially it reminds us of the *Critique of Pure Reason,* which begins with space and time and then goes on to the categories; but Kant derives the categories not from space and time but from an independent source, namely, the logical table of the judgements. And Kant does not think, as Alexander thinks, that empirical things are as it were visibly stamped with the categories; on the contrary, he thinks that the pervasive characteristics empirically discovered in the world of nature are not the categories themselves but the schemata of the categories. Thus, to take one example, what we empirically find in the world of nature is never causality or the necessary connexion binding effect to cause, but only the schema of causality, namely, uniform sequence. The schemata are the pervasive characteristics of the visible world; they depend upon space and time, being simply forms of spatio-temporal structure; and when we ask whether the categories in

Alexander's system are in Kantian language categories or schemata, the answer is easy and can be verified by anyone from Alexander's pages: they are not categories, they are schemata. It looks as if Alexander, deeply influenced by Kant but resolving at all costs to avoid Kant's subjectivism, had cut out the Kantian categories altogether, because they are merely subjective necessities of thought, and contented himself with the schemata by themselves. But if you cut out the category of cause and substitute its schema, you are cutting out the idea of necessary connexion and trying to content yourself with mere uniform succession; that is, you are attaching yourself to an empiricism like that of John Stuart Mill, for whom a cause simply is an antecedent, and for whom consequently all knowledge is mere observation of fact, devoid of any apprehension of necessity. And this is precisely what Alexander does. His theory of knowledge amounts to this, that minds are things which have the power of knowing other things; and his carefully expressed theory of philosophical method is an application of the same doctrine, for he tells us that the business of philosophy is not to reason or argue or explain but simply to observe and describe facts.

This strain of empiricism is the weakness of Alexander's philosophy. If the method of philosophy is purely empirical, if the universal merely means the pervasive, the necessary merely the actual, thought merely observation, a system built on this method can have it in no driving force or continuity; there is an element of arbitrariness in every transition, and a reader who stubbornly asks, '*Why* should space-time generate matter; *why* should matter generate life; *why* should life generate mind?' and so on, will get no answer; he will only be told that he must not ask such questions but must accept the facts in a spirit of natural piety. Yet if the child is father of the man, surely the first duty of natural piety is to respect, and endeavour to satisfy, the childish tendency to ask questions beginning with *why*.

In its extreme form this weakness appears in Alexander's exposition of the idea of God. That exposition is dazzling in its austere splendour; but this must not blind us to its paradoxical character. Our ordinary thoughts of God are no doubt childish; but, such as they are, they begin by thinking that in the beginning God created the heavens and the earth. Alexander.

on the contrary, says that in the end the heavens and the earth will create God. The crudity of this contradiction is modified by making God an equivocal term, and saying that in virtue of its nisus towards the emergence of Deity the world may be called God, as it were, by anticipation; but Alexander is not entitled to that ambiguity, and his real thought is expressed by another passage in which he says that God, being a qualitied infinite, cannot exist (which must imply that His existence is intrinsically impossible, so that He never *will* exist); God, he says, is therefore only a picture, but a picture eminently worth drawing, though nothing actual corresponds to it (or, we must add, ever will correspond to it). Hence, when Alexander asks himself whether he can support the belief, common to religion and traditional cosmology, that God is the creator of the world, he replies that on the contrary he must reject it: it is space-time which is the creator and not God: and strictly speaking God is not a creator but a creature. This conclusion would not be objectionable in a philosophy whose method claimed to be one of rigid deduction; for such a method, if it arrived at conclusions contrary to ordinary ideas, would be entitled to defend them by argument (as Spinoza defends his view that our ordinary idea of freedom is an illusion); but in a philosophy whose leading methodical conception is that of natural piety it *is* objectionable, for such a philosophy ought to take current ideas as it finds them, and nothing is more essential to the current idea of God than the belief that He created the world.

Thus in spite of the brilliant merits of Alexander's work—one of the greatest triumphs of modern philosophy, and a book where no page fails to express truths illuminating and important—there is a certain gap between the logic of the system and the materials, derived from his general experience as a man, which he has tried to work into it. According to the logic of the system, Alexander ought at the beginning to deny logical necessity and fall into pure empiricism; at the end he ought to deny God and fall into pure atheism (except in so far as he would identify God with space-time). And both these steps might easily be taken by followers less richly endowed than himself with experience of life and thought; clever philosophers, unlike him in not being great men. The alternative way of following him is to reconsider the logic of the system, and in especial to reopen the question whether categorial characteristics pervading nature as a whole do not imply something outside nature, something prior to space and time.

This brings me to Whitehead; not because he is a follower of Alexander, for he is not; but because he represents a view, in general very much like Alexander's, in which that question is differently answered.

§ 2. *Whitehead*

Whitehead's early training was that of a mathematician and physicist. He approached philosophical studies first in the capacity of a mathematician reflecting on his own thought, collaborating with Russell in *Principia Mathematica*, a vast treatise on the logic of mathematics which laid the foundation of modern logical analysis. Later he wrote books giving a philosophical account of physics: *The Principles of Natural Knowledge* and *The Concept of Nature*, and finally, in 1929, a general metaphysical system: *Process and Reality*. His work in philosophy forms part, and a very important part, of the movement of twentieth-century realism; but whereas the other leaders of that movement came to it after a training in late-nineteenth-century idealism, and are consequently realistic with the fanaticism of converts and morbidly terrified of relapsing into the sins of their youth, a fact which gives their work an air of strain, as if they cared less about advancing philosophical knowledge than about proving themselves good enemies of idealism, Whitehead's work is perfectly free from all this sort of thing, and he suffers from no obsessions; obviously he does not care what he says, so long as it is true. In this freedom from anxiety lies the secret of his success.

His theory of nature much resembles Alexander's. Nature for him consists of moving patterns whose movement is essential to their being; and these are analysed into what he calls events or occasions, which correspond with Alexander's point-instants. But, unlike some who have adopted his analytic method, he refuses to believe that the real being or essence of a complex thing is discovered by analysing it into the events of which it is composed. Analysis does indeed reveal the components, but it disintegrates their structure; and Whitehead shares Alexander's view that the essence of a complex thing is identical with its structure or what Alexander calls its pattern. By the more fanatical realists the analytic method has been welcomed chiefly as an escape from subjective idealism. In actual experience the known object is always found coexisting with the mind that knows it; and subjective idealism argues that this whole composed of two parts, the knower and the known, cannot be split up into its components without damaging both of them by taking away from each something that it possesses only as united with the other. Therefore, argues the idealist, things as we know them would not exist precisely as we know them if they were not thus known. To this argument the analytic method seemed to provide an answer: a complex whole is merely an aggregate of externally related parts, and analysis reveals those parts as they are, in their separate natures.

This argument against idealism is valid only if it can be maintained, as a perfectly general proposition, that every whole is a mere aggregate of its parts. This, however, was not maintained even by G. E. Moore, who used the argument against idealism; for Moore also admitted that there are what he calls organic unities, that is, wholes having characteristics not referable to any part separately but only to the whole as such. Moore recognized such unities especially in the field of ethics. It may have been a recollection of Moore's principle which has led Whitehead to describe his own philosophy as the philosophy of organism; for what he has done is to regard that principle not as a somewhat strange and paradoxical law holding good in ethics and perhaps in some other fields, but as a universal principle applicable to the entire field of existing reality. He is quite explicit as to this universality of application. Everything that exists has for him its place in what he calls the order of nature (*Process and Reality*, II. iii); this order consists of 'actual entities' organized, or organizing themselves, into 'societies': thus every actually existing complex thing is a society, and Whitehead says 'a society is more than a set of entities to which a class-name applies; that is to say it involves more than a merely mathematical conception of order' (p. 124). Here Whitehead strikes at the root of the doctrines which lead some of his former colleagues to make such assertions as that a chair is the class of sense-data which would commonly be called aspects of the chair.

When Whitehead constantly asserts that reality is an organism, he does not mean to reduce all reality to biological terms; he only means that every existing thing resembles a living organism in the fact that its essence depends, not on its components merely, but on the pattern or structure in which they are composed. Hence (to point out just one obvious corollary) it is idle to ask oneself whether the rose really *is* red or only *seems* red to our eyes; the same order of nature which contains the rose contains also human beings with their eyes and their minds, and the situation which we are discussing is a situation in which roses and men are equally real, and equally elements in the society of living things; and its colour and its beauty are real features of that society, not simply located in the rose (that is what Whitehead calls the 'fallacy of simple location') but located in the society of which the rose is one organic part. Consequently if you put to Whitehead the realist's shibboleth, the question 'Would a rose be red if there was nobody looking at it?' he would answer very mildly 'No; the whole situation would be different'. And consequently strict members of the realist faction regard Whitehead with suspicion, as a wobbler.

Nature, for Whitehead, is not only organism, it is also process. The activities of the organism are not external accidents, they are united into a single complex activity which is the organism itself. Substance and activity are not two, but one. This is the basic principle of Whitehead's cosmology, a principle grasped by him with unusual tenacity and clearness, and taught to him, by his own account, by modern physics with its new theory of matter. The process of nature is not a merely cyclic or rhythmical change, it is a creative advance; the organism is undergoing or pursuing a process of evolution in which it is constantly taking new forms and producing new forms in every part of itself.

This cosmic process has two main characteristics, which I may call, using Whitehead's own words, 'extensiveness' and 'aim'. By 'extensiveness' I mean that it develops upon a stage of space and time: it is spread over space and goes on through time. By 'aim' I mean that Whitehead, like Alexander, explains process in terms of teleology; the A which is in process of becoming B is not merely changing at random, but orientating its changes towards B as a goal. *Qua* extensive, the process implies what Alexander calls space-time; Whitehead calls it the extensive continuum, and argues very much like Alexander that it has both a time-aspect and a space-aspect, but that without space there could be no time and without time no space. Like Alexander, too, he holds that there is not, and never has been, any empty space or time, devoid of pattern and process; the idea of empty space-time disappears when the traditional concept of matter disappears and is replaced by the concept of process. And the finiteness of the natural world both in space and time—the spatial limitations of the starry universe and the temporal limitations of its life—are explained by Whitehead's conception of cosmic epochs. He observes that there are many pervasive characteristics of nature which are arbitrary: for example, the quantum of energy, the laws of the electromagnetic field as discovered by Clerk Maxwell, the four dimensions of the continuum, the axioms of geometry (*Process and Reality*, pp. 126–7: I give his own examples). He argues that since there might have been worlds where these arbitrary characteristics had different values, our world is only one among many possible worlds, as Leibniz argued before him. But unlike Leibniz he holds that, since there is no intrinsic reason why these other worlds should not exist (for if there were, they would not be possible worlds, but impossible worlds) they must all exist, not here and now, but elsewhere in space-time, and his general name for them is cosmic epochs.

The finiteness of a particular cosmic epoch means not only that, since the laws which define it are arbitrary, there might be and therefore must be and therefore are others outside it in space and time. It means also that, since the laws which define it are arbitrary, they are not perfectly obeyed, from which it follows that the order prevailing in any given cosmic epoch is shot with instances of disorder, and these instances of disorder gradually subvert the order and turn it into an order of a different kind. Here are Whitehead's own words (*Process and Reality*, p. 127):

'But there is disorder in the sense that the laws are not perfectly obeyed, and that the reproduction [by which new electrons and new protons come into being] is mingled with instances of failure. There is accordingly a gradual transition to new types of order, supervening upon a gradual rise into dominance on the part of the present natural laws.'

Qua teleological, or pervaded by aim, the cosmic process implies something else, and here we come to the difference between Whitehead's cosmology and Alexander's. For Alexander, the new qualities which emerge when a new pattern forms itself in space-time belong to that pattern and nowhere else; they are in every sense new, wholly immanent in the new event in which they are realized. For Whitehead, they are in one sense immanent in the world of existence, but in another sense they transcend it: they are not mere empirical qualities of the new occasion, they are also 'eternal objects' belonging to a world of what Plato called forms or ideas. Here Alexander inclines towards an empiricist tradition—I have already pointed out his affinity, in such matters, to John Stuart Mill—which identifies that which is known with the fleeting sense-datum of the moment; Whitehead, with his mathematical training, represents a rationalist tradition which identifies that which is known with necessary and eternal truths. This leads Whitehead back towards Plato, and to asserting the reality of a world of eternal objects as the presupposition of the cosmic process.

Alexander's cosmic process thus rests on a single foundation, space-time; Whitehead's on a double foundation, space-time and the eternal objects. This difference enables Whitehead to solve certain fundamental problems which for Alexander remain necessarily insoluble. Why, for example, should nature have in it a nisus towards the production of certain things? For Alexander, there is no answer: we must simply accept the fact in a spirit of natural piety. For Whitehead, the answer is that the peculiar quality belonging to those things is an eternal object which, in his own phrase, is a 'lure' for the process: the eternal object, exactly as for Plato or Aristotle, attracts the process towards its realization. Again, what is the relation between God and the world? For Alexander, God is the world as it will be when it comes to possess that future quality which is deity; but, as I have already said, this makes nonsense of the ordinary meaning which we attach to the word 'God'. For Whitehead, God is an eternal object, but an infinite one; therefore He is not merely one lure eliciting one particular process but the infinite lure towards which all process directs itself. I quote his words (*Process and Reality*, p. 487):

'He is the lure for feeling, the eternal urge of desire [remember that feeling and desire, as Whitehead uses the words, belong not exclusively to minds but to anything, so far as it is engaged in creative and therefore teleological activity]. His particular relevance to each creative act, as it arises from its own conditioned standpoint in the world, constitutes him the initial object of desire establishing the initial phase of each subjective aim.'

Whitehead, following out his own train of thought, has thus reconstructed for himself Aristotle's conception of God as the unmoved mover, initiating and directing the entire cosmic process through its love of Him. And it is curious to observe that the identity of his own thought with Aristotle's, which Whitehead gladly admits, had to be pointed out to him by a friend, Whitehead having apparently never read Aristotle's *Metaphysics* for himself. I mention this not to ridicule Whitehead for his ignorance of Aristotle—nothing could be farther from my mind—but to show how in his own thought a Platonic cosmology may be seen, in the pages of *Process and Reality*, turning into an Aristotelian. Thus the cycle of cosmological thought in the modern world, from Descartes and Newton to Whitehead, recapitulates the cycle running from Thales to Aristotle. But this recapitulation is not a mere repetition; it has taken up into itself first the body of Christian theology, and secondly, derived from that theology, the body of modern science, the new physics of the seventeenth century and the new biology of the nineteenth. In Whitehead's work all the leading conceptions of these new sciences have been fused into a single view of the world which is not only coherent and simple in itself but has also consciously connected itself with the main tradition of philosophical thought; Whitehead himself, though he shows no sign of having read Hegel, says in the preface to *Process and Reality* that in his ultimate views he is approximating to Bradley and the main doctrines of Absolute Idealism, though on a realistic basis (it is this that shows his ignorance of Hegel's polemic against subjectivism), and claims continuity with the philosophical tradition. Whitehead has escaped from the stage of thinking that the great philosophers were all wrong into the stage of seeing that they were all right; and he has achieved this, not by philosophical erudition, followed by an attempt at original thought, but by thinking for himself first and studying the great philosophers afterwards.

The main lines of Whitehead's philosophy, I have said, are coherent and simple; but in trying to think them out one is confronted by several difficulties of a secondary but very important kind. I will try to state the most important of them, making it clear at the same time that I am not always sure whether Whitehead himself has confronted them or not; for he is always a very difficult writer to read, and even after long study one is often not sure how far he has solved by implication problems which he appears to have ignored.

First, then, concerning the theory of eternal objects. He seems to think that everything which Alexander would call an empirical quality—the blueness of the sky at a particular moment, or the relation between two musical chords never written in just that way before—is an eternal object. Certainly that is the express view of Santayana, with whom Whitehead here claims general agreement (*Process and Reality*, pp. 198–9). Now, when once the doctrine of eternal objects is allowed, it seems only logical to extend it in this way *à outrance*. The classical passage on this subject is in Plato's *Parmenides*. Are there, Parmenides asks, forms of right, beauty, and good? Certainly, says Socrates. Are there forms of man, fire, or water? Socrates replies that he is not sure. Are there forms of hair, mud, and excrement? Certainly not, says Socrates; though he admits that the denial lands him in difficulties out of which he can see no way. The meaning of the passage is clear enough: some things must be regarded as eternal presuppositions of the cosmic process; others may be regarded as its products, and perhaps only as its products; others are merely its by-products, not even necessary or intelligible in themselves, but intelligible (so far as they are intelligible at all) only as accidents in a creative process whose true products lie elsewhere. Alexander would regard all these alike as products; Whitehead would regard them all as presuppositions. Socrates, when he tried to adopt Whitehead's view, was put to flight, as he says, by fear of falling into an ocean of nonsense. By this he certainly did not mean that it would be distasteful to attribute anything so solemn and awful as an eternal form to anything so mean and unpleasant as the smell of dung; he meant that a world of eternal forms which included in itself forms of every empirical detail in nature would only be a lumber-room of natural details converted into rigid concepts, and that a world of forms so conceived, instead of explaining the processes of nature, would be a mere replica of these processes themselves with the process left out.

There is one way in which this absurd conclusion could be avoided. If it could be shown, for example, that the form of the good, in itself and quite apart from any temporal process in nature, implied the form of animal as its logical consequence; if it could be shown that this form of animal implied in itself the form of excrement; then it could be held that there were forms of these things, and that in their logical connexion and logical subordination they did really serve to explain the processes of nature. In other words, the heart of the problem is the question how the world of eternal objects, the realm of essence, is organized in itself. Plato certainly saw this, and Hegel saw it; but if you are going to take that line, as Whitehead seems to do and Santayana certainly does, you saddle yourself (as Hegel did) with the terrible task of logically deducing every empirical quality to be found in the world from some absolute first principle, or else giving up the attempt to take seriously the doctrine of eternal objects. For there is nothing to be gained by merely insisting that the sky now has this peculiar blueness by participating (as Plato put it) in the form of that shade of blue, or, as Whitehead puts it, by the ingredience of that shade as an eternal object in the present occasion of my seeing the sky; by saying that, you are appealing to the conception of a world of forms or eternal objects as the source or ground of natural process, and you must go on to give an account of this world and show why that shade of blue appears in it.

Santayana is ready with his answer to this demand; but it is an answer which I think would not appeal to Whitehead. If I ask Santayana to show that this shade of blue is an essence logically implied by his general conception of a realm of essence, he replies that 'no essence can have implications': 'implication is something imposed on essences by human discourse, leaning not on logic but on the accidents of existence' (*Realm of Essence*, p. 81). Hence, for him, every essence is completely self-contained and atomic; the realm of essence is simply an aggregate or structureless congeries of details. This, unless I am very much mistaken, is simply the ocean of nonsense which Socrates was so anxious to avoid; and it certainly could not be attractive to a mathematician like Whitehead, whose training is chiefly a training in grasping the implications of essences. But how Whitehead would answer the question I do not know.

The second main problem which Whitehead seems to leave unsolved concerns the creative process of nature. Evolutionists like Lloyd Morgan, Alexander, or General Smuts believe that this process passes through definite stages: that there was a time when no organic life existed on this planet, and that it arose, upon an inorganic physico-chemical basis, through the working of the creative process itself. But this does not seem to be Whitehead's view. In *Nature and Life* he treats inorganic nature not as a real thing which once existed by itself and still exists as the environment of life, but as an abstraction, nature itself conceived apart from the vital elements which everywhere pervade it. He asks what we mean by life, and having defined it by the three marks of self-enjoyment, creative activity, and aim, he goes on to argue that all three are really present in the so-called inorganic world, though physical science, for its own perfectly legitimate purposes, ignores them. Now this seems to me a way of avoiding the problem rather than solving it. There are types of process which occur in living things and do not occur elsewhere; Whitehead's three marks do not seem to me an adequate account of them; and what he has done is to escape the difficulty by restricting the connotation of the term 'life' to something which does indeed belong to life but is not its differentia but only the genus common to itself and matter. Consequently he falls back into the very subjectivism he is trying to avoid, by calling matter a mere abstraction. There is an element of truth in this conclusion, but it requires a good deal more working-out before it can be regarded as satisfactory. If matter is a mere abstraction, we must ask, what are the real facts in nature which oblige us to make that abstraction?

The same difficulty arises in connexion with mind. The characteristic mark of mind is that it knows, apprehends reality. Now, says Whitehead, this too, like the characteristics of life, is nothing really unprecedented. Everything enjoys what he calls 'prehensions', that is to say, somehow absorbs what is outside itself into its own being. An iron filing prehends the magnetic field in which it lies, that is, it converts that field into a mode of its own behaviour, responds to it; a plant prehends the sunlight, and so on. The peculiarity of what we ordinarily call 'minds' is that they prehend an order of things which no lower type of organism can prehend, namely propositions. Here again there is profound and important truth in Whitehead's view; his refusal to regard mind as something utterly disparate from nature, his insistence that mind as we know it in man is something that has come to be what it is by developing functions belonging to life in general and even in the last resort to the inorganic world, is altogether admirable; but once more, as in the case of life, he is on the horns of a dilemma. Either mind is at bottom the same as these elementary prehensions, in which case there is no creative advance, and life is a mere abstraction from mind as matter is from life, or else it is also something genuinely new, in which case we have to explain its relation to that out of which it grew. And once more Whitehead does not appear to see the dilemma. No one has more vividly realized and described the resemblances, the fundamental continuity, running all through the world of nature, from its most rudimentary forms in the electron and proton and the rest of them to its highest development known to us in the mental life of man; but when we ask him whether this series of forms represents a series really developed in time he seems uncertain of his answer; and if we go on to ask the precise nature of the connexion between one form and the next, he has no answer to give except to insist that in general all such connexions are formed by the creative process which is the world itself.

§ 3. *Conclusion: from Nature to History*

I have traced in this book, as well as my ignorance and my indolence have allowed me, not indeed the whole history of the idea of nature from the early Greeks to the present day, but certain points concerned with three periods in that history about which I happen to be less ignorant than I am about the rest. And having reached a sort of ending, I must close with a warning and a question. The warning is that the ending is not a conclusion. Hegel, nailing to the counter in advance the lie that he regarded his own philosophy as final, wrote at the end of his treatise on the philosophy of history, *Bis hierher ist das Bewusstseyn gekommen*, 'That is as far as consciousness has reached'.

Similarly, I must say now, 'That is as far as science has reached'. All that has been said is a mere interim report on the history of the idea of nature down to the present time. If I knew what further progress would be made in the future, I should already have made that progress. Far from knowing what kind of progress it will be, I do not know that it will be made at all. I have no guarantee that the spirit of natural science will survive the attack which now, from so many sides, is being made upon the life of human reason.

The question is: 'Where do we go from here? What constructive suggestions arise from the criticisms I have brought, however timidly, against the conclusions of Alexander and Whitehead?' I will try to answer it.

Throughout the long tradition of European thought it has been said, not by everyone but by most people, or at any rate by most of those who have proved that they have a right to be heard, that nature, though it is a thing that really exists, is not a thing that exists in itself or in its own right, but a thing which depends for its existence upon something else. I take this to imply that natural science, considered as a department or form of human thought, is a going concern, able to raise its own problems and to solve them by its own methods, and to criticize the solutions it has offered by applying its own criteria: in other words, that natural science is not a tissue of fancies or fabrications, mythology or tautology, but is a search for truth, and a search that does not go unrewarded: but that natural science is not, as the positivists imagined, the only department or form of human thought about which this can be said, and is not even a self-contained and self-sufficient form of thought, but depends for its very existence upon some other form of thought which is different from it and cannot be reduced to it.

I think that the time has come when we should ask what this other form of thought is, and try to understand it, its methods, its aims, and its object, no less adequately than men like Whitehead and Alexander have tried to understand the methods and aims of natural science, and the natural world which is the object of natural science. I do not think that the defects I seem to have noticed in the philosophy of these great men can be removed by what may be called the direct route of starting according to their own methods from their own starting-point and doing their work over again and doing it better. I do not think it can be done even by starting from their own starting-point and working by better methods. I think that these defects are due to something in their starting-point itself. That starting-point, I think, involves a certain relic of positivism. It involves the assumption that the sole task of a cosmological philosophy is to reflect upon what natural science can tell us about nature, as if natural science were, I will not say the only valid form of thought, but the only form of thought which a philosopher should take into account when he tries to answer the question what nature is. But I submit that if nature is a thing that depends for its existence on something else, this dependence is a thing that must be taken into account when we try to understand what nature is; and that if natural science is a form of thought that depends for its existence upon some other form of thought, we cannot adequately reflect upon what natural science tells us without taking into account the form of thought upon which it depends.

What is this other form of thought? I answer, 'History'.

Natural science (I assume for the moment that the positivistic account of it is at least correct so far as it goes) consists of facts and theories. A scientific fact is an event in the world of nature. A scientific theory is an hypothesis about that event, which further events verify or disprove. An event in the world of nature becomes important for the natural scientist only on condition that it is observed. 'The fact that the event has happened' is a phrase in the vocabulary of natural science which means 'the fact that the event has been observed'. That is to say, has been observed by someone at some time under some conditions; the observer must be a trustworthy observer and the conditions must be of such a kind as to permit trustworthy observations to be made. And lastly, but not least, the observer must have recorded his observation in such a way that knowledge of what he has observed is public property. The scientist who wishes to know that such an event has taken place in the world of nature can know this only by consulting the record left by the observer and interpreting it, subject to certain rules, in such a way as to satisfy himself that the man whose work it records really did observe what he professes to have observed. This consultation and interpretation of records is the characteristic feature of historical work. Every scientist who says that Newton observed the effect of a prism on sunlight, or that Adams saw Neptune, or that Pasteur observed that grape-juice played upon by air raised to a certain temperature underwent no fermentation, is talking history. The facts first observed by Newton, Adams, and Pasteur have since then been observed by others; but every scientist who says that light is split up by the prism or that Neptune exists or that fermentation is prevented by a certain degree of heat is still talking history: he is talking about the whole class of historical facts which are occasions on which someone has made these observations. Thus a 'scientific fact' is a class of historical facts; and no one can understand what a scientific fact is unless he understands enough about the theory of history to understand what an historical fact is.

The same is true of theories. A scientific theory not only rests on certain historical facts and is verified or disproved by certain other historical facts; it is itself an historical fact, namely, the fact that someone has propounded or accepted verified or disproved, that theory. If we want to know, for example, what the classical theory of gravitation is, we must look into the records of Newton's thinking and interpret them: and this is historical research.

I conclude that natural science as a form of thought exists and always has existed in a context of history, and depends on historical thought for its existence. From this I venture to infer that no one can understand natural science unless he understands history: and that no one can answer the question what nature is unless he knows what history is. This is a question which Alexander and Whitehead have not asked. And that is why I answer the question, 'Where do we go from here?' by saying, 'We go from the idea of nature to the idea of history.'

INDEX

Aaron, 33.
acoustics, Pythagorean, 52, 146, 159.
Adams, J. C., 177.
Aëtius, quoted, 33, 37.
Alexander, Samuel, 83, 147, 167–8, 169, 171, 173, 175, 177.
— empirical strain in his philosophy, 163, 169.
— his conception of the evolutionary process, 159–61.
— his cosmology discussed, 158–65.
— space-time and the categories in, 162–3.
— weakness of his conception of God, 163–4, 169.
analogy as the basis of cosmology, 8–9, 19–20.
Anaxagoras, 18.
Anaximander, 33–5,36, 37, 38, 39, 41, 42, 50, 51, 59, 99.
Anaximenes, 35–40, 41, 42, 50, 51.
anima in nature, 101.
animism, 3–4, 31–2, 95, 147.
Aquinas, St. Thomas, 5.
Aristophanes, 82.
Aristotle, 93, 128, 156, 170.
— his cosmology, 24, 76, 80–92, 94, 96, 97–8, 99, 123, 124, 155, 169.
— — theology, 87–91, 99, 115, 170.
— *intellectus agens* in, 116.
— on activities which take time, 19–20, 146.
— — causality, 75, 84.
— — history of early Greek thought, 29, 30, 31, 32, 33, 34, 35, 39, 49, 55, 61, 65, 66.
— — matter, 91–2, 95, 125.
— — meaning of φύσις, 45, 80–2.
— — movements, 20–1.
— — Plato, 55, 61, 65, 68, 72, 122.
— — Socrates, 65, 67, 68.
— — theory of knowledge, 85–7, 117.
— *Politics*, quoted, 24.
— theory of the soul, 6.
Arunta, the, 33.
astrology, 96.
atomic theory, 18–19, 92, 142–3, 145–7.
atomism, Greek, 98, 153, 155.
Augustine, St., quoted, 37.

Bacon, Francis, 93, 100–1, 107.
baroque', 4.
Bentley, Richard, 143.
Bergson, Henri, 10, 147.

Bergson (*contd.*)
— his cosmology discussed, 136–41.
— creative evolution, 138.
— dualisms in, 137.
— inadequacy of his philosophy, 140–1.
— reduces nature to terms of life, 139.
— difficulties of this reduction, 139–40.
— vicious circle of his cosmology, 140.
Berkeley, 7, 102, 117, 130.
— failed to solve problem of relating infinite and finite mind, 115–16, 122.
— G. E. Moore's misinterpretation of, 8.
— his conception of nature as mind's work, 113–14, 123, 139.
— regarded mind as the only substance, 114.
— solved correctly the problem confronting him, 114–15.
biology, autonomy of, 133.
— controversies in, 136.
Boethius, quoted, 97.
Bradley, F. H., 170.
Brahe, Tycho, 98.
Bréhier, E., quoted, 29.
Broad, C. D., 8.
Bruno, Giordano, 5, 98–100, 106.
Burnet, John, 47–8, 81.
Bury, J. B., 10.
Butler, Joseph, 9.

Caesar, 25.
Calvin, 96.
Campbell, Lewis, 58.
cause', meaning of, 75–6.
— and principle, dualism of, 100.
choice must be reasoned, 40–1.
Christianity, 8, 77, 93.
Christian theology, 87–8, 115, 170.
Cicero, quoted, 33–4.
classical physics, 23.
— — controversies in, 144–5.
concordance in Greek music, 52–3.
condensation and rarefaction, 36, 37–9, 51, 73.
Copernicus, 5, 95, 96–8, 99, 115.
Cratylus, 61, 65–8.
creation, Christian idea of, 32, 77, 163–4.
Croce, B., quoted, 4.
Croton, 49.

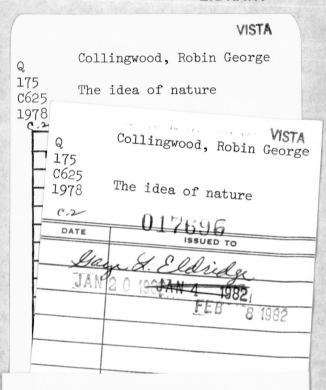